Richard Voorhees Risley

The Sentimental Vikings

Richard Voorhees Risley

The Sentimental Vikings

ISBN/EAN: 9783743312586

Manufactured in Europe, USA, Canada, Australia, Japa

Cover: Foto ©ninafisch / pixelio.de

Manufactured and distributed by brebook publishing software (www.brebook.com)

Richard Voorhees Risley

The Sentimental Vikings

The Sentimental Vikings

BY

R. V. RISLEY

JOHN LANE
THE BODLEY HEAD
NEW YORK AND LONDON
1897

To
E. F. C.

CONTENTS

	PAGE
THE SWEEPING OF THE HALL	1
AN INCIDENT	37
WHERE THE WOLVES DANCE	61
THE SACRILEGE	99
THE STORY OF THE OAR-CAPTAIN	115
THE LAST VOYAGE	145

THE SWEEPING OF THE HALL:

AN OLD DANISH TRAGEDY

THE SWEEPING OF THE HALL

AND now this is the story of Witlaf the harper, that he told in the great hall of Gorm, the king of all Denmark, ten centuries ago, waving his handless arms in the flickering glow of the firelight.

I tell the tale of Snorē, the lord of the north of the island of Zeeland, years ago; and of how he swept his hall as the day broke.

First, as to his birth. Men say that the heavens were darkened, and that tumultuous clouds swept low over the battlements, and that voices were heard, meaningless, in the air. I do not know—wonders are kind to great names when they have been memories a little time.

But this much is true, that we in the hall of the castle were told by a white-faced woman, just as the sun set—I remember how red its light fell on the rush-covered floor, and how the woman leaned half through the door and told us, holding the curtain—that the child was born, and was strong, and a man; but that the mother was dead, and that the Lord Sigmund was with her.

That night in the hall, by the light of the fire, as we men were talking in whispers, and telling kind deeds of our lady (for she was ever about in the cottages, and she and her women made soft-sewed clothes for all the men of the ship-crew), came, from behind the curtain that is to my lady's chambers, a long, low wail of a child, strong and insistent, and then a man's tread for a few paces, and then silence again, save for the men's whisperings and the sound of the squeaking of their leather-belts as they moved, and the gentle rubbing of the wooden shields on the walls as the wind blew through under the rafters.

And afterwards, when the fire burned low, the men departed for their beds and left the hall empty, and then I also went, because I did not like the shadows, but to the battlements, not to my sleep, for I felt that this night meant some-

The Sweeping of the Hall

thing, and I was not yet enough settled in my mind to lie and think in the darkness. So, lonesomely, I paced the battlements, while the moon rose, and all around me lay the great forest reaching almost down to the edge of the moat, and throwing its shadows over the silver water and on the white walls of the house. And in the distance, the long, still, snake of the fjord stretched out under the moon, till it curved and a black point of trees cut it off suddenly.

And at last, when the woods had become dusky, and the distant water where it passed out of sight was grey instead of silver, and then slowly turned to pink, I went down the steep stairs, through the yet dark galleries, where the carving on the corners was worn so smooth and stained with smoke—down to the chill, dark hall, and, kneeling on the hearth, built up and lit a fire of good beech twigs among the ashes, while the first day of the life of Lord Snorē, who swept this same hall of his at another dawning, broke through the long windows and shone on the armour.

6 *The Sweeping of the Hall*

There are truer ways of reckoning time, O king, than by the indifferent passage of the meaningless years. Some moments, of the flying of a thought in length, fill more space in our lives and memories than much of everydays.

Yet something remains to me of those light-footed years till I see again clearly. Thus, I remember Lord Sigmund, my Lord Snorē's father, set forth that year after the grain-planting was over, and until it was tall, he sailed the high seas, and brought back white furs from the North, and stories of mountains and ice-floors.

Next, I remember a strange ship come rowing one day up the fjord, and of her landing, and the men coming up to the hall, where they stayed many days; and of how they ran in the fields, shouting, and throwing the grass at each other; for they were sea-weary.

Then they departed, and there passed some more seasons and harvests, with sometimes hunting of bears or of deer, and the hewing of pieces of woodland.

Thus the years trod by softly while the Lord Snorē grew to his manhood.

The Sweeping of the Hall

And Lord Sigmund would sail away with his men every spring when the planting was over, and my young lord would sit in his place in the hall, and, when need was, give justice unto the townsfolk. Good years, O king, when the fields grew wide, and the board was filled for a hundred men who sat there every evening.

When, looking back from where I now sit—I hope near the end of my life—I see again clearly, it is the time of midsummer in the meadows that stretch by the side of the fjord, where the woods fall back, an hour's boat-row from the castle. There, just when the still noonday drew to its close, and the slanting sun was beginning to throw its afternoon brightness in our brown faces, my Lord Snorē and I lay stretched out in the long, sweet grass, he with a heavy crossbow—a new weapon then—and the carcasses of two brown deer lying beside him, I idly talking and ever looking forth over the blinding waters for sight of his father's ship that we might begin to expect now, the grain being tall,

Suddenly, from behind a point of jutting woods round which the fjord ran curving, grew and took shape a something long that the sun shining on made painful for the eyes—a long, low something that, curving in again, glided between me and the dark green point of trees. It was the ship! The young lord sat up on the grass, and putting his hand on the carcasses of the deer, rose to his feet. "It moves too slowly," he said. It was true. Now we could see the swing of the oars, and the pause between the strokes was very long.

"Look at the dragon," he said again, shading his eyes with his hand. I saw now that the great beak that had used to be so fierce in its red-and-gold painting was broken off, so that only its curving neck rose from the bow. And, looking again, I saw that the sides of the ship were battered, as if by rocks, and that many of the oar-blades were broken and tied to their stems with ropes. I ran to our boat that lay against the side-of-grass, and hurriedly tumbled its stone anchor on board.

"He must have sunk the other ship or he would have come home in her," I said, shipping the steering-oar.

Lord Snorē raised himself from the bottom of the boat where he had been stooping to place the two deer, and turning his shaggy head, looked at me curiously. "I will sit in my own right now!" he answered.

Beneath the lord's long strong strokes the sharp-prowed skiff went rapidly over the still water, and now we could see the broken dragon's-neck and the rents in the shields hung over the sides more plainly. We were almost within the shadow of her mast when a tall man—I knew his face for that of Esbiern the oar-captain—with a great red cloth round his head, leaped on the bow, waving his long arms wildly and shouting to us over the sunny waters, wild words of some sea-fight.

Our prow cut the shadow; half-unwilling hands reached over the gunwale to grasp our boat; we clambered over the side and turning, we looked along the length of the battered ship, over the half-empty rowers' benches, past the pale faces of five or six men with linen-swathed heads and arms—on, over the confusion and wreckage that littered the centre of the ship, to where, leaning against the edge of the fore-deck, lay the body of Sigmund the lord with the half of the crew of his returned ship arranged in a long sitting row beside him.

So, with Lord Snorē at one of the big oars to help the weary men with one more rower, and I heaving on the great steering blade and guiding the ship slowly over the shallows, we went silently up the fjord through the afternoon.

That night, when the men and the household were done eating and only the horns and wooden tankards of beer stood along the board, my Lord Snorē spoke from the great seat where he sat moodily, with his fist on the table, and the chair-cushions thrown on the floor beside him; and thus he spoke, with the men leaning silently forward to hear him:

"The men of the ship have told ye of the fight; how in the south, off Lolland, they met a Viking-ship which attacked them. How they fought and drove

The Sweeping of the Hall 11

the Viking; how that the Viking led them along the coast till, our men weary with rowing, there came two fresh ships from a bay, hidden, friends of the Viking; and how that Lord Sigmund died in the fight, and how that our men fled north, while the Vikings shouted; and our ship ye have seen!

"On the sixth day after this, at the sun-rise, let the ship be ready with new oars; the ship's men will stay here to rest. I shall take the men that I call my guard; those who hunt bears with me in the forest. But let the dragon's-neck remain broken."

This he said, and the men were silent, the old ship's crew sitting, looking dejectedly along the board, their ale undrunk, and shuffling their feet in the rushes. Then there was drinking one to another while the women took down the men's axes and armour-coats from the walls and carried them off to their houses to clean them; and there was laughter and boasting and talking loud making up courage, and some got up from their places and went seriously out of the hall to the houses and to their children, and some talked to the men of the ship's crew.

Thus the evening passed, and the men went home to their beds early, save for a few who sat down with made-up indifference and talked, while their beer-mugs stood on the benches till they grew warm in the firelight.

So the next six days we worked and made ready, hewing and smoothing new oars, and whetting our knives on the grind-stone; and at sun-rise on the sixth day, with a long crowd of men and women on the strand and the rain pouring down out of the misty brown sky, we hauled our ship down the beach and setting ourselves in our places rowed splashingly away from the castle; while the fine rain ran down our faces and the shouting grew faint in the distance.

And so passes that part of my tale and I take up the second.

Now there come two months, O king, that are as difficult to see clearly as the length of a flame in the sunshine.

The Sweeping of the Hall

We sailed south to Lolland, but we could find no word of a large ship with a plain prow and a new crew.

And we landed on many shores, and much I learned of the art of minstrelsy.

And Lord Snorē managed his men well and was a kind lord over us, though fierce, and long of anger.

We sailed, passing along the coast, sometimes running so near that the coolness of the trees was grateful to the sun-burned men — where we could see the bottom over the side of the ship, as we glided, stilly, over the white stones that glimmered through the clear water.

And sometimes we would pass by grey castles with small villages and houses over the fields, where the people would come out and look at the ship, and when they saw the broken dragon and that it was a ship for fight, run in again, or hurry towards the castle from the fields. Then we would call out to them to go back to their oxen, or to go on with their thatching, and wish good marriages unto the maidens, and laugh at them while they stood staring.

And we would land sometimes and hunt in the forests; and then we would cook our meat all through over great fires, and not eat it half-fresh as on shipboard.

Once we chased a great ship and came up with her, but on calling out, we found they were Northmen; and the ship that we wanted was of our own race. So we gave them some rope in exchange for some leather, and drank "skaal" to them over the bulwarks as they spread their brown sail going northwards.

Sometimes we landed at some lord's castle, sending a man before that they might know us as friends. And here were we entertained for many days, and were well liked, both on account of the kindness and manhood of my Lord Snorē and on account of the sturdiness of the ship's men, and on account of the quest we were on.

Sailing thus, O king, come I to that part of my tale when the ladies smile, and when the lords in the hall look away and seem not to listen—yet would I be prompted if I forgot it.

Now, my Lord Snorē was a fierce man

of manner and face, being very large, with his shaggy head held high on great shoulders—a man more for fighting and combat than for young women's eyes— and old ones' tongues.

Yet like some ugly men he seemed the manlier by his ugliness.

We sat in the hall of Lord Rudolf of Lolland, anxiously waiting the coming of the ship of his brother, gone Viking— hoping for word of the ship we had searched for. And Lord Snorē hunted and rode with Lord Rudolf every day, till it came to the evening that he had set for departure.

And, drinking health to the lord, as he raised his great mug to his lips, I saw his eyes glance over the edge, and they met the eyes of Lord Rudolf's fair daughter. And I saw a slight surprise come into his face; it grew into amazement; and he drank the cup slowly still looking at her.

We stayed many days at Lord Rudolf's.

It was when the men were growing weary of waiting and the household that eat in the hall knew all of my songs— when the keel of the ship was fast grounded—that one night as I lay asleep with my back to the bulwark I felt a hand shaking my shoulder. And, as I grasped his arm in the darkness, Lord Snorē's voice came to me whispering:

"Awake; and come out of the ship, silently—here in the darkness," he whispered, as I came over the side and let myself drop by my arms to the sand.

I saw that he was dressed in his armour, and had his great axe in his hand, as he pulled me into the shadow of the steering-oar, where it stuck over the stern, its blade of broad silver where it shone to the moon-light.

"Do you hear the noise up at the castle?" he whispered.

"It is surely Lord Rudolf's brother returned," I answered when I had listened; for a sound like the grounding of swords and the tramping of men passing in and out over the drawbridge came to me, faintly, from where lay the castle beyond the black line of trees: the night was very still.

"Nay, it is not that," whispered Lord Snorē, looming up dim by the ship's side: "Listen, Witlaf: I love Lord Rudolf's daughter—ah! so thou knowest?—and this night have I gone up to look at her window where the light is—nay, listen—and as I was standing there dreaming, I think, sudden and soft her voice came to me out of the darkness, from just within the great window that is at the side of the hall, and looking up, I heard her call to me gently, saying, 'Snorē, Snorē; come here to the window-ledge, silently—quick! Back to your ship, Snorē—my father is arming himself in his chamber; I heard the clang of his armour: he is angry because that I—love thee. The castle is filled with his men, and—I love thee!'"

And the lord's great hand was raised in the darkness.

"Now, Witlaf," he whispered, and I heard his voice tremble, "the maiden is safe in the ship; but thou knowest," and his voice grew firm, "that the half of our men lie drunk on the fore-deck—and 'tis hard to move ship with so few. Say, Minstrel, wilt thou hold the ship while I, with the rest, warm my hands at the castle?"

And thus it was that I, the harper of Lord Snorē, came to be sitting in the moonlight inside the ship, with my harp by my knee, and my axe in my hand, and a pale-faced maiden beside me who listened in silence to the distancing tread of my lord and his men as they stealthily passed up the path towards the castle.

So, seemingly for years and years, we sat there, with the water lapping against the side of the ship, and the sound of the straining of leather and the shuffling of feet as the men sleepily put on their arms on the fore-deck. Then, more years passed, and the maiden shivered and crept closer, and I put my great skin-cloak around her.

So we sat and waited; and the moon sailed grandly overhead throwing flakes of white on the dancing water to seaward; and save for the lapping of water and occasional sounds from the fore-deck, there was stillness—out of which an owl cried, thrice, with its long, strange, mournful note, and then ceased; leaving the silence more silent.

Then, suddenly, from out the darkness, seemingly miles away, there rose, and rose, and hung on the air, and slowly died away, a great cry in a man's voice. Then there was silence once more for a moment. And now began a confused dull rabble of sound that I knew well enough; with a skin-moving swish in it like the whetting of knives. And there were far sounds of voices, and sometimes a curious hollow drubbing, like a hammer on the side of a ship; this, I could tell, was the sound of my Lord Snorē's great axe as it beat on the door, and when it ceased presently I knew that the door was down.

Now, for a long time only the far sounds and the occasional voices came to us; and the years grew long again, and I heard the water lapping against the side of the ship.

Suddenly, out of the darkness and into the strip of moonlit beach that lay between the edge of the black forest and the silvery ship, came running a man, silently, and swaying as he ran, and just mid-way in the moonlight, he stopped, ran round uncertainly twice in a little circle, and then pitched forward with his face in the sand and lay still. The maiden by me gave a little cry and hid her face on the edge of the bulwark. Then we waited again and listened to the barking of dogs in the distance; and so more years passed, and the lapping of the water grew loud again.

Now began to come wounded men in pairs, stumbling groaningly over the side, and soon with these began to come back other men out of the darkness, unwounded, but bloody enough, and these waited in a little crowd outside the ship panting, and wiping the sweat from their foreheads, and leaving the prints of their hands on the planks where we found them next morning. And, last, with a little knot of unwounded men around him, came Lord Snorē walking heavily, swinging his axe, with the blood dripping from his shaggy foretop and from the ends of his hands. He stood while the men slowly shoved off the ship, then plunging through the water like horses and splashing it over their red armour and faces, they all came clambering aboard, and throwing off their steel hoods and sword-belts, sat them down to the oars to get the ship out of shoal water. But my Lord Snorē came to the gunwale, and taking the maiden's hand drew her to him, wrapped in the great wolf-skin, and lowered his head on her shoulder.

Thus we left that shore; and when far out, we saw first a flicker and then a glow of fire, and the burning of Lord Rudolf's castle lit up the sea, and we heard the cocks crowing over the water as we turned our prow homeward, while the oar-blades rose and fell, dripping silver.

Now, as we sailed homeward the maiden was given the after-part of the ship, save for the steersman, and because, that, loving Lord Snorē, she was afraid of him; yet ever looking towards the forward part of the ship where he sat with his men: thus she would have me come and harp to her and tell her sagas and tales; and she told me many things in return.

And then Lord Snorē would come to the edge of the raised deck and leaning upon it, talk to her, while my harp made low music.

In the years that have passed, O king, a mist like the autumn mist that lies white on the earth in the morning has grown between my eyes and the past, so that only the hill-tops break through it.

22 *The Sweeping of the Hall*

Now, I will tell of the passing of Snorē and Helga, and like the scenes of a play, the last scene of my tale is the bloodiest—for fighting was the half of men's lives in those days — thank the Gods! So, to the end of the tale.

As we rowed up the fjord past the meadows and woodlands, the oars making song on the oar-pins for gladness, pointing out things to each other, my lord and I talked over his taking of Helga to wife on the morrow; my lord laughing loud and resting his hand on my shoulder and glancing back ever at Helga as she sat looking out on the fields. We arranged that all the men of his land should be called in for the great feast that night at the castle, and that the feast should be until daybreak, when he would take Helga as wife before all men. Then these things being arranged, my Lord Snorē went to her and told her, and she answered him honestly blushing a little that she was glad; and then bade him sit down beside her, and tell her of

The Sweeping of the Hall

what we were passing. And thus, with Lord Snorē sitting beside her pointing out woodland and meadow, and the men smiling up at them, as they rowed in the waist of the ship, we came to the strand and the old castle stood before us; and landing we pulled the ship up on the beach and with the crowds laughing and welcoming us and all confusion, we all went up to the castle. I remember till now, the great comfort it was to get fresh boots and clothes, and new harp-strings, and soft cushions to sit on.

It was a great feast that night! The long hall with the smoke-stained walls, hung with great boat-shields and bright arms, with skins of bear and deer, and with branches of green oak and beech leaves.

Down through the whole length ran the long table, loaded with meat and drink, and from the cushioned bench where sat Snorē and Helga, to the other end of the table, were laughing and welcoming. And from the fire at the end of the hall, where two deer swung, cooking and burning, in the blaze, and from the great candles along the gay walls came yellow light shining on arms and laughing faces.

And the smell of the cooking deer came through the hall, and the cakes of brown meal were piled up on the end of the table, and the great mugs rang as the drinking men struck them together, and the voices and laughter rose loud in the hall. And then the men rose, shouting, to my lord, and drank welcome and "skaal" to him; and, standing, they drank a great welcome to my lady, and the mugs came down with a crash on the board, and the shouting was long ere it rested. Then my lady spoke from the place that she held by Lord Snorē and thanked them in woman's words; and they roared again in their gladness.

After, they called to me for a song. Then I stood up and sang to them with my harp; I sang of peace, and of the glory of it; and of battle, and of the strong joy of it; and of welcome, and so again peace. And the men stood,

The Sweeping of the Hall

shouting, unto my lord, till the hall rang with it; and the great fire roared, and the yellow light flashed on the arms and the faces, and glowed on the painted shields hung on the walls—oh it was a great feast!

And now, O king, this is the last scene of my play—all this was long ago, and these loves and these lives have passed away utterly.

It was far in the night and the empty platters and dishes were piled on the floor, and the men were drinking the frothing beer, resting their mugs on the foam-dripping board or on the empty seats of the drunken, who lay around the sides of the hall asleep on the rushes; the arms were thrown in the corners with dishes, and the air felt chill ere the dawning in spite of the piled-up fire.

Now Helga being weary arose, and leaned towards my lord Snorē to kiss him ere she went to her chamber, and I who sat by the side of my lord, looked up at her, smiling; for she had never kissed him before among men. And looking, I saw, ere their lips met, a change come into the eyes of Helga and she stood still. Then, making a little gesture as of casting something away from her, she stooped again, but the change grew in her eyes and she could not. I followed her look to where it rested on the curtained door that enters the hall from the apartments which face on the water.

Slowly I reached for my axe, and leaning to look at my lord as I lifted up his, I saw him waiting expectantly, shyly before his men, for Helga's good-night. So I leaned a moment. Then I whispered to him, and put the axe in his hand.

The great table is overturned, the broken stools and benches lie over the floor, the fire is scattered, and the flying ashes drift in the smoke and swirl around the heads of the combatants, making them cough as they strike. The drunken men along the walls are stabbed or trampled among the torn rushes, and the foe that have stolen in through the seaward windows are pressing over the benches.

We are behind the upturned table, and

fighting desperately, our backs to the wall. The enemy rush against the table but the long arms of our men drive them back. I am holding a boat-shield from the wall over Helga and using my axe with the other hand.

Lord Snorē is sweeping the space in front of him clear; he has thrown aside his shield. We seem to have been fighting for hours in the dim hall.

Our men begin to fall behind the table; they are in their leather coats, and guard badly in the murk.

The swords clang on the edge of the table; the men stumble over broken dishes. I see through the smoke one of them with his foot fast in a wooden beer mug. They run along the table striking. The smoke comes in my eyes, and the forms grow dim.

Now they go back leaving us, and a tall man dressed in strange armour, breaks through them, and stands, banging his leg with his sword.

"I am Swend, kinsman of Rudolf of Lolland; and I came and found his hall ashes. Say, dost thou think that a ship with the dragon beheaded, can sail where it will and no man be the wiser? And who was it, think you, that drove your ship—laughing?" And he stood, snarling and digging the floor with his swordpoint, like a wolf in his anger.

Then Lord Snorē, resting his axe on the table—"If thou art the man who fought with my father and called two fresh ships to thy helping then I am glad thou art come to my feast in my hall!"

Then Swend—"Thou hast murdered thy host for the sake of his daughter! I, his kinsman—" and he stopped while the smoke swirled down and I heard him coughing.

"Who would have been kinsman to me had I slept in my ship, Rudolf's guest? And the maiden chose freely. He would have bit on my axe-blade—though he were Odin!" And Lord Snorē lifted his axe, shouting aloud in his anger.

I hear Swend yell to his men through the smoke; the floor shakes as they come running towards us. They break out of the gloom; they leap on the table smiting and stabbing. But the long arms of

The Sweeping of the Hall

our men pull them down; they fall. Lord Snorē's axe swirls and bangs on their armour; the table is cleared. They draw back, gasping like dogs; their wounded lie against the wall in the drip of the candles. I see the chests of our men heave in their weariness. They lean with their backs against the wall, wiping their slippery hands on the skirts of their garments. The smoke comes down; again they come. The fight closes in again the struggling forms striking over the table, I catch dim sight of swift grey shapes and the flashing of swords high in the air. Our men are panting like bulls; I hear the straining of their leather coats as they lean, striking into the mist. Bodies of men come shocking against the table; there is roaring, and trampling of feet, and banging and clashing of armour, and breaking of wood, and the sound of Lord Snorē's axe falling regularly comes through the darkness.

All this comes to me, dimly, as though through a dream, and dreaming, I catch a passing sight of the shadowy figures in the smoke on the other side of the table. The fight goes on; it goes on for ever and ever it seems; and the world in the smoke and the noises and sounds of the combat grow farther and farther away; they come to me unreally, in a far-off roar, like the sea.

I hear the sound of waves; the water roars, and roars, and roars—farther and farther—then nearer again; the ship moves and heaves and turns slowly round under the motion. And now I hear the sound of my harp playing, coming through the sound of the water; that ceases, and I hear the sound of Snorē's and Helga's voices speaking softly. I hear the words —they come to me over the continuous sound of the water—and they are silly words, about a piece of her hair that she has given him—and I laugh—

And my laugh awakens me, sounding ghastly under the dull smoke; and the tumult and ringing and roar of the combat springs up around me again.

And now, over the banging of metal and the clashing of armour on armour and the sounds of the trampling and breaking of wood and the howling, comes another sound—surely my Lord Snorē's axe! But the blows are so quick, there is something awesome, unnatural, in the blows of a man falling so fast.

And now I am aware of a change that has come in the fight. I no longer see the ghost-figures passing, dim in the smoke. The sound of the fighting comes from out in the hall. I wait, peering into the smoke. Slowly it lifts from above the table—lifts, growing dimmer.

Outlines come out of the distance. The opposite wall of the hall looms up into the darkness. The candles glimmer and show through the smoke. I look down the hall. A grey mass, moving indistinctly, and the sound of a great continuous crashing coming from somewhere within it.

The smoke lifts more; bodies of men on the floor come out, and I can see the dim tapestries waving on the walls; and now the great sound of the crashing comes louder.

The smoke lifts yet more, it is pouring out of the windows and under the roof; the walls spring out into distinctness; and I see, plain, the end of the hall.

32 *The Sweeping of the Hall*

A crowd of men struggling and falling over each other against the great door; the flashing of armour, swords thrown in the air, clenched hands raised and falling, the end of the hall full of tumult of arms and legs and bodies, as the men rush and surge over each other against the outlet.

But, dominating all in its hugeness, striking the men before it, making a glory with its flying axe—enormous, irresistible, clothed in red, seeming to shake the air with the roar through its skin, yet utterly silent—Lord Snorë, gone mad with the combat, striking with the strength of a falling tree—sweeping out the hall before him!

The door is open! The men pile up on the threshold; the door grows high—is darkened—is full. Grows open—men whirl along the floor under the axe—the wave breaks, it recedes, it runs away into the corners, it dissolves and runs away in foam—the door is empty.

The last of the smoke rolls around under the roof, the walls rock with the reverberation, and the sounds of our voices calling to one another are lost in the echoes. The hall heaves, the sounds die, going out with the smoke under the roof; and the pale light of the daybreak falls through the long windows. The candles gutter and go out, falling down from the walls, from the burned-out spikes. We stumble over the table, on, over the broken benches, and over the bodies.

It was a good fight, O king, when Lord Snorē swept his hall! There is now but little more to tell. We found a great figure standing idly by the door when we came there; it was swinging a great axe in its hand, with its head sunk on its chest, and it swayed when a man touched it, and fell back limply into our arms.

As they carried him up the hall towards the great bench a white figure ran past me.

Then the lights went out, the world heaved, and I fell down across the table; for both my hands had been cut off upon its edge.

When next I saw the hall, having come back out of the long unreality that had lasted so many days, the first snow of the winter lay on the window-ledges and the great fire was blazing merrily. I remember how strange it all looked. And there, walking up and down slowly, and leaning on my lady who guided him, was the wreck of a great man who grasped weakly for support at her robe. I went up to him and stood silently. My lady touched me with her hand and whispered to me to speak to him. Then said I to my lord with a strange softness in my throat: "I hope my lord is better—after his sickness." And he answered, "Yes, yes—yes, yes—yes, yes—" nodding his head, sillily. And then my lady led him to the great bench, and, seating him, talked to him child-talk and tended him gently.

That night, as I sat by my lady, silent, the boy who fed me having gone away to the others, one rose, and thinking to please me I suppose, brought me my harp out of an inner room.

I think we were all glad when my lord died at the last snow. Then my lady used to go among the cottages of

The Sweeping of the Hall

the villagers, tending those who were sick, talking with the young girls, and comforting all who were in any sorrow. The women used sometimes to cry when she spoke to them. And in about three months after we buried my lord, when summer was come again, and the sun had already begun to warp the timbers of the ship on the beach, when the boys ran shouting in the shallows, died my lady also, and we buried her by the side of my lord.

Then left I the castle; and men tell me that it is pulled down to build more houses for the villagers, and that the old ship has mouldered away on the beach and can no more be seen.

And all this happened years ago and is forgotten. If some one will hold my cup I will drink "skaal" to the king that he has listened.

And this is the tale of the sweeping of the hall, that the old minstrel used to tell at the board of King Gorm, waving his handless arms in the glow of the firelight.

AN INCIDENT

AN INCIDENT

THE great fog lay dun over the sea, and the shadows moved over the motionless ship, passing swiftly; yet there was no wind.

We lay wrapped in the wood-ashes coloured air, through which the mast shone glimmering in many lines when you looked at it, idly swinging under no wind. Easily the water slipped by, dimly streaked, through the cloudy vapour. The men from the stern could not be seen by those in the bow.

We yawned and stretched ourselves, the peculiar smell of the fog rising into our nostrils. The warm air lay like the weight of a cloud on our foreheads, and we grumbled wearily, wanting a sight of the sun.

While we waited thus sighing, out of the dun vapour on the right came a cry indistinguishable. After we had been on our feet for some moments, there came the swift wash of oar-blades, and their rabble on the gunwale, going very fast.

Then the sound of a far-away crash, and, after a little, clinking as of knife on glass, and a dead murmur of voices in the fog.

We straightened ourselves, and after a moment of hesitation, my lord gave the word to get out the oars, which we did very gladly though with little noise, pulling carefully, our mast-top lost in the shifting roof. Very soon we could hear the sound of the fighting coming quite plainly over the dusky sea; and in a little time thereafter, we saw, while the vapour swirled back for a moment, three brown hulks near together. We lay on the edge of the foam-touched space of water, catching occasionally glimpses of the moving shapes: only a large piece of wood floated past us.

Have you ever listened to a fight at sea? The men were leaning over the bulwarks, their hands on their axe-handles, their feet grasping firmly the deck. My lord raised himself in a moment; we ran swiftly along the water

An Incident

under the quick, ragged stroke, the ships rose before us, we swept past the side of the largest one, dropping the oars.

The man next to me leans back suddenly just as my bow twangs; arrows strike into the bulwarks.

Fierce faces and bent bows send their sound of shouting and twanging at us over the close side of the enemies' ship. We thrust with our oars that slip along the timbers; the arrows sing and streak past, their long feathers grey like storks.

Then the ship by us turns off into the fog with a dash of oars that sends the white spray flashing for a moment; it is a shadowy form in the mist; a tall brown thing disappears beside it; we are alone on the smooth water with the ship we have come to help.

The hillside is sprinkled with flowers, the setting sun draws our attention from them. "Come," says Lord Erik to my lord, "let us go in." They walk slowly over the darkening blossoms.

"Ever since you called out to me through the fog," says Lord Erik, "and came on with me and became my guest, I have trusted you with all that I care, or think, or am, and you have never before told me of this."

My lord smiled rather sadly at the handsome, eager, young face, where the emotion of disappointment lay, like all emotions on those expressive features, bare.

"We do not always speak so easily of what we like," he answered.

"Oh, it is like an old sail you speak of her—why do you not care?" And the beardless mouth went down. "Does she not like you?" glancing at my lord's strong limbs.

"Perhaps; girls do not usually love old men," my lord answered, looking kindly, amusedly, at the boy.

"You old! You are not old! I think of you as something with me, you——"

"Try your success with women, my son," broke in my lord laughing; "you, a young lord—come."

They went in.

A word about us. We were Eastern men from the island; my lord, old, burned-out, — though not with years, — restless — deliberately — silent, kind, secretive, and wise in some old-gained sad kind knowledge of men. So we had cruised where my lord was quiet, seeming content, till in the fog opportunity brought us new friends, at whose sunny, lonely town we were guests. When my lord had told his host of the woman to whom he was betrothed, idly, we men who stood by watching noticed them keenly, for we were interested in my lord and the why of his choosing the maiden. She, the daughter of a timid lord, her mother dead—a fair thing who gave flowers to boys in fun.

This is what we were.

Now, whether it was the beer we drank that night, or whether the long rest — though I think the long rest — the men began to speak in loud voices with sea-tales. Now, the young lord, his slim right hand on the great mug, laughed to my lord: "Let us go and make some sea-tales!" and laughing, raised his mug to his lips, glancing merrily at his guest over the top as he drank.

"But your ship," said my lord looking at him.

"Let us go in yours, mine is too battered," answered young Erik. "Ah—that was a joy—the fog and the shouting and the grey ships!"

His face grew pale in the light with excitement. My lord seemed reluctant.

"Yes"; he said. "Where shall we go?"

"There—here—anywhere!" cried young Erik, jumping to his feet and waving his beer-mug to three points of the horizon.

"The men in my town will take care of the harvest."

We were at sea again; my lord cynical on the after-deck, young Erik talking to the men.

We were passing a sand-spit that ran out into the calm water just touched with ripples. Over the top of the sand we saw masts rising, and came out into the open again, where we could see the yellow over our sides through the light green water, the sand-spit falling behind —we saw three great ships, heavy-masted, long-yard-armed and with sharp prow.

An Incident

These slowly neared with flapping sails, and we could see that the decks were crowded with men. They passed by, as they went hailing us in rough tongue, laughing out many-languaged questions as to where we had come from.

Then came something that was very strange. A few men and myself saw my lord very slowly take up a cross-bow and drawing it, deliberately shoot an arrow into the side of one of the nearest ships. A yell of defiance came over the water, and young Erik cried to every man to take his arms.

Why had my lord shot that arrow? Who can say? We do not know.

They came down on us singing Icelandic songs, as is the custom of most of these people, for the ships were principally full of these men.

One ship passed close by us and the men shouting over the sides, threw spears at us as they went by, brushing us with their oars. Then this ship rounded on behind us, and the spears came in showers over the stern.

But part of our men, dropping their

weapons, and throwing themselves at the oars, drove us over the sparkling sea, toward the ship that came gliding toward us, with a howl from the enemy that reverberated in the ears of the straining men inside our wooden bulwarks, our long prow cut into their ship's side. I saw their mast bend away from us. The other ship now came on, singing.

We shoot at her with our long-bows, and the singing is turned to shouting as they come toward us. My lord shouts to pull on the right-hand oars and while some of us tug wildly the others shoot over the side. Slowly we turn, and the heeling ship before us comes into view over the bow — slowly we turn, as the third ship nears us. We move round, and, their arrows in our faces, they go sweeping by—just by—the oars grazing.

And now we can see the ship we have run down as she turns over her deck to us; the men tumble down the rowers' benches; they leap into the water; she settles sideways, the water bubbling.

Now come the two other ships from behind us.

An Incident

Young Lord Erik lies wounded on the after-deck. Half of the men sit white, about the arrow-struck mast. The other two ships come on.

My lord cries to face them, and we move slowly, seeing over the bow the ships rush on over the place where their comrades sank, striking the heads of the swimming men with their oar-blades.

We drop our arms and, heaving three times on the long-oars, send our ship between the other two.

A flight of arrows, a glimpse on each side of a passing mast — they are behind us. My lord calls from the after-deck, "Row away, row away!"

Turning my head to look at him I see him laughing, the bow still in his hand.

We rowed round the sand-spit, and as we went round it we saw the two ships close together picking up men from where a mast stuck up out of the light-green water.

"It is the second time we have been comrades," said young Lord Erik, his right arm bandaged, gazing up palely at my lord as they stood by the rail.

My lord smiled.

"Yes, true," he said.

We were running along a forest-covered strand, where the roots of old trees gnarled themselves into the water.

"Now we must go to the hall that I told you about," said my lord.

"Yes and see the girl I am so eager to see!" exclaimed young Lord Erik, his white face lighting as he gazed up smiling to my lord.

He laughed.

"Ah," he said, "it is both pleasant and good," and he gazed along the depleted seats.

The next day there was a strange excitement in my lord's eyes, and we began to put together our clothes. And late in the afternoon we came into the little bay on the shore of which lay old Raud's castle. We ran through the water hauling our ship up with cables, and with shouting from the people coming welcomingly down from the castle, we hastened up the beach.

As we sat over the meat that night, a

curtain was pulled aside from the door by
Lord Raud's chair, and he, rising feebly,
my lord slowly, and smiling, and young
Lord Erik jumping to his feet eagerly,
we saw her come gliding in whom we
had seen often before. She gave her hand
timidly, yet with a little laugh, to my
lord, shyly yet kindly to young Lord Erik,
and welcomed them as her guests as her
father had welcomed them as his at the
castle-door as we passed over it. How
such a maiden could be the daughter of
such a feeble, timid, dainty old man as
Lord Raud, I could never know. As a
child pretending to ask for forgiveness
was her face—half-laughing and half-sor-
rowful. Her moving was like a ripple of
blown cloth, it was so springing grace-
ful. And her eyes, when they occasionally
looked at you, had a woman's innocence,
never a man's straightforwardness.

It was sun-set three days later. Walking on the beach I could see my lord and
Hildur pacing slowly, he laughing, along
the grass that stretched by the path to
the houses in the wood. The scene was
lit up by one of the sometimes far-reach-

D

ing clear sunsets of autumn. I could see her hand raised in remonstrance, and though I was too far, I could see that they were both laughing. Presently she nodded her head of gold hair to him, and turned into the castle-door, leaving him alone in the soft, far, unusual, light. He turned.

As he moved, I saw that he was not laughing. As he came down to the beach, I could see the same excitement in his eyes that had always been there when he came near her, since his hair began to grizzle, and she used to bring the cynical old father's friend his beer in the great hall after meat — a little maiden.

He passed me and turning at a word behind me, I saw him meet young Lord Erik; smiling again. But the young man's face was troubled, that face on which all emotions were like shadows on even water.

Not a word, after my lord's greeting, passed.

Suddenly, my lord called to me over his shoulder:

"Lord Erik wishes to go home, wilt thou take ship with him and come back to me?"

Their figures were dim in the lessened light.

"Let another man go; I stay. Send one of the younger men," I answered.

My lord held out his hand to me. Young Lord Erik's face was white in the dusk.

Over our beer, by the fire-light, I could see the glances Hildur threw to young Lord Erik, I could see his hard-shut mouth; I could see my lord's cynical smile and the gleam of the excitement in his eyes; I could see old Lord Raud, daintily fingering his beer-mug-handle— thoughts far away. And I was glad I had stayed by my lord.

So, the next day young Lord Erik went north with the ship. And my lord stood on the beach smiling gaily and called out gay words of next summer. And the young face brightened for a moment as the ship drew away.

Well, all that day I followed my lord about, smiling at his gay moods, quiet when he forgot — which gave me pleasure. I am sure he tried to leave me behind him sometimes, after mid-day, by fast walking, but I came. And toward evening, as we tramped back along the beach to the hall, I coming behind, my lord turned, and started running. In a moment I caught him; and he bent suddenly over my shoulder, with a sound like a seal grunting. So, I held him for a moment till he shook himself into himself again and walked up towards the castle, I falling back again; we never said anything about this.

Now I go out on a long ending, that is only true. After some days of silent smiling on the part of Hildur—to me she looked very ugly—and much laughter—which cheered old Lord Raud—on the part of my lord, he asked Lord Raud to give him the maiden now, for he was anxious to take her away. So my lord spoke to her about it, and she said yes.

Then we went away; and old Lord Raud stood on the beach, our ship being back, and large tears came down from his eyes. So we all went home again and took the maiden with us.

There is little use in telling a tale of

An Incident

women. Yet some scenes rest with me that concern my lord, so I tell it all. Thus those two used to walk past the door of the hall, and past again, while I stood in the doorway; and I would hear what they said, for my lord did not care for me, and it was very loving. But after it was over he would go down to the water and look out, and stretch his arms, and yawn—then break in with a laugh and walk back again.

Often in mid-summer came ships, and their men were well fed and liked us.

Hildur used to be gay now only when these ships would come; in the winter she was silent.

The house was badly kept; many times I have made rough sowing for my lord, so that he would not know.

When spring came and the sea was bright at the early morning, we would often get drunk in the hall toward night after standing watching the glancing of little waves through the lazy day. I used to put water in my lord's beer that he might not drink too much. He never used to speak of young Erik now;

of which I was glad; he was only a boy.

So the spring went by and the green of the leaves grew darker and the sunlight lingered over the sea till late. There were no good dishes in the hall, and the women who cooked never thought of the things my lord liked. Hildur would go to her chamber early, and we all would wander out along the sea-shore, away from the clatter of dishes the women made. And when it grew dark we would come in and sing over great beer-tankards; but we loved the beer better than the soon-died-out singing.

We were weary in the sunshine, and old sea-sagas came to us so easily. The women were cross, and children cried, instead of running about in the forest. I do not know what is in man, or how himself works on himself; we are parts of the woods, the sea, the far light. The spring was running into summer; the free air in the night made us gasp like tired dogs, and we felt smothered.

That night my lord sat on a piece of rock overlooking the sea, I was behind him. All in front of us was dark, but we could hear the sound of the water come from away and all along the coast.

Then, out of the silence that lies under the world, came over the edge of the sea, the bare, silver, edge of the moon, lighting slowly the tips of the waves. No mist around her; the unroofed, upward depths of the sky, full of suspended stars, that seemed to wink, being alive. She rose out of the sea, reaching toward us the elves-bridge she carries, over which we cannot see the spirits pass; sending out her still beckoning that she sends to all men. The little waves danced joyously in the light; there was no sound at all from the shore, only the water whispering on the sands.

My lord sat black, in the moonlight. After a while he got up and returned toward the shadowy hall.

He went in and took a great tankard of beer from my hand and drank, then turned toward me.

"The beer is warm—too warm," he said. "What a beautiful night. The beer is too warm." He waved his hand with one of his old indifferent gestures, his mouth trembling. I filled him another tankard of beer; he drank it at a drink and then asked for another, this he also drank and threw himself down on a bench. "Drink!" he said, "drink!" laughing loud.

I drink with him again and again. He leans back on his bench laughing. "Ah, old war-follower!" he cries, his voice ringing strange in the empty moonlit hall. "Dost thou remember our first cruise? We took the battleship! and that other; where we were caught in the ice. Dost thou remember Lord Raud? Ah! that was a grand time. And when we chased the bears in Lord Snore's forest. Through all our cruises; that old ship off Norway that we chased and frightened so? See the moonlight!" he said, suddenly, and stopped laughing. Then, with a wave of his long arm, he leaned back and called out again. "Jolly war-dog! Ah!—another tankard; Skaal! Skaal! to our old times! Skaal! Ah! Old war-dog! It is not good for men to put their hearts on women. They find them empty; there is no water in an unfilled pitcher—better the old seashells, like us, that are always filled. Do you know," and he started up and shook his beer-tankard in the moonlight, a tall figure, "that, since I was a young man, I have loved that woman! She was a little ——Be silent! A ghost comes!" He grasped my arm.

There, gliding in all in white through the door at the side of the hall came Hildur like a spirit in the moonlight. She spoke from where she stood, and our delusion of a spirit was scattered. For she spoke cross, empty words, as she stood by the disorderly hearth complaining of neglect.

I stood by my lord's bench, and I saw the old excitement come into his eyes. She went on complaining; beautiful in the moonlight. My lord raised his tankard and took a long drink, then with the same old cynical laugh, he stood there; and she stopped. Then my hands gripped the back of the bench, for my lord, still laughing, threw the empty tankard at her with all his force. I saw her lie white in the moonlight. So that is ended.

The next day we buried her, who had died from a fall from the hall-terrace to the rocks beneath. And in the after-mid-day, we sailed in our ship, past the green woods. We sailed north to young Lord Erik's town, and found him married, and happy with kisses and things. So we sailed away again laughing at this easy consolement, and my lord was very gay at the pleasure of the sea.

Soon the men were brown, and the sun shone above level waters, and we sailed lazily past dense woods.

Thus one day, as we landed to cook our meat under the trees, one of the men thought he saw a glance of armour away off in the forest. But thinking it was only the sunlight on one of the beech-trunks, we cooked and sat down to our meat.

They came running out of the forest, trying to break past us to get to the ship. There was clank of swords on armour, and the smoke from the fire wavered from its straight column; then, they drew back. Their chief came from the beach-reaches now, and laughing said

An Incident

they had lost their ship, so, seeing ours, had tried to rush into it, and get away before we could beat them off.

So we asked them to sit and have meat with us, and they sat down; though we were careful of our arms till they had eaten.

And the next day we landed them at a town, where they might build another ship.

This is the tale of the marriage of my lord just as it happened.

WHERE THE WOLVES DANCE

WHERE THE WOLVES DANCE

THREE years before, in the winter time, I had brought my wife Elsa from her father's, loving her as fools and lonely men love dogs and women. So I kept ever near her, but was shy of her. Now this is the tale of a very strange thing, and it begins from her. Though my hall stood far to the west on the main, where even the sight of the sand-hills could be found from the highest tower, yet there were trees and gardens on the other side, and paths ran down to little ponds, and cattle browsed over rich uplands and sheep grew fat. There were sixty men in my hall; heavy men and slow, but slow to change, and as their fathers leant before them, so they leant also from the worn castle windows, and the window-sills were smooth with the rubbing of their elbows. As to the hall and its build, there is little need be said. It was square and large, and partly of stone, with a banquetting-hall, and enough of small rooms and of cellars for the storage of meat and milk and beer. In the summer sometimes I would go down to the coast, and crossing in my ship over to Fōen, buy cattle or grain or go to the south ports for some strange rare thing for my lady; thus it was for three years, and contentment had grown round me like a woof.

So one day a horseman came riding slowly. He bore to me a message that three of the priests of the Lord-Bishop of Lund demanded shelter that night under my roof. I was standing dressed in my best leather suit and with my handsomest sword-belt by my chair at the head of the table, when the door swung open and they entered. They came slowly up the hall into the light, and lifting their heads when they came to the bottom steps at the top of which I stood, they showed the faces of three old worldly men, fed on the follies and the agonies of man. They were all pale and stooping, but the one to the right, a tall man with one shoulder higher than the other, bent the most, and leant upon the shortest priest, who was in the middle.

"Greeting," I said; "you are most welcome."

They advanced up the steps and the tall old priest stepped towards me and blessed me in a low voice, and then asked to be shown to his room. I conducted him myself, leading the way to the apartment with a candle, and the two others followed, their arms crossed over their chests. Thus came the learned Father Cefron into my house. Next morning the two other priests departed in haste, the way they had come, to inform the Lord Bishop of Lund that the learned Father Cefron was ill and like to die, which indeed seemed to be true. I sat by his bedside as he lay with his face to the wall, his shaven head looking dark against the bed-clothes.

"When will he come? When will he come?" he would murmur; then clenching his hands and turning towards me and sticking both fists out, "I want the boy," he said; then flinging his face to the wall impatiently. This kept on for two days, till I sent a messenger to the one of the two priests whom I had liked most (the fat one), asking who he, "the boy," was, and telling him how the learned Father Cefron lay calling for him and would not be quiet. In eight days there came back my messenger, saying that he, the boy, would follow on, and would probably be at the hall to-morrow morning early. So it was. While I was yet in bed I heard the barking of dogs in the courtyard, and the cracking of whips, and the voices of the men calling to one another, and the clatter of their wooden shoes on the stones. I sent word that he should at once be taken to Father Cefron if so be that Father Cefron was awake; and he went quickly and I did not see him at all till after noon that day. Then, as I rose from my meat—the men had already trooped out of the hall, their dinner over—there entered through the tapestried door a tall, broad-backed, narrow hipped, slim-limbed, youth, who held his head high, and bore eyes full of laughter under his wild light hair.

"My Lord Olaf," he said, extending

his hand, "I ask your pardon for coming late to my meat; but good Father Cefron has wanted me with him. I have been much with him since a child, you know."

I welcomed him as a guest should be welcomed, and called for more meat to be placed before him and some ale; but the ale he only sipped and I sent to the back of my cellars for some bottles of Southern wine, which he liked much better and thanked me for, and which I liked him the less for liking better than the ale. When we had drank and eaten, we rose, and taking my arm, he walked with me up and down the end of the hall.

"Old Father Cefron," he began, "is a learned man, but a man who has kept too strictly within the rules of his order; he lacks blood, therefore he lacks heart; he has only a head, but that head is one whose like will not be seen in Skandinavia again in this century"; and the youth's voice was touched with enthusiasm. "Now why it is I do not know, but having killed the man in him over ponderous books, he feels he must have me to put some laughter in his life, and give him something human to think of for the moment when he is tired of the battles and treaties and that of dead kings; therefore it is, my lord and host, that I would venture to ask of you as Father Cefron has asked me to ask of you—indeed has commanded—that you let me stay with him here in the castle till the term of his life is ended, which seems not very long."

So young Heinrick became one of my household, and though I never liked him for his dainty ways and foreign prettinesses, yet I became used to him, and his figure was familiar on the edges of my fish-ponds, in the corridors of my hall, and was seldom absent when the time for eating came. He seemed to be much with Father Cefron in the early evening, and I could hear Father Cefron's groans come from his chamber sometimes when I passed by the door; and he was good at wrestling tricks, and quick to a wonder at southern fence, yet I liked him none the better, and I could see that the men liked him neither, for they would not learn his wrestling tricks till pressed almost to command, and I could see them whispering and glancing after him as he passed by. By this time my Lady Elsa and myself lived as most loving people. I would take her to the fish-ponds, and she would scream and find delight in the excitement; or sometimes she would come to meet me through the wood with some of her women and some men to follow, and I would come making the wood hoarsely musical through my curved horn, and bring her deer from the uplands and great hares shot with crossbow, and sometimes little birds, very hard to come near, which dwell among the sand-hills to the westward; then she would always have flowers in her room; in the winter evergreens and the mystical, bunched, mistletoe, and ever my favourite meats and green things, cooked or wild, all the year were before me.

It was as the winter came on that I fell ill and the fever came into me; and after lying for three days I tried to get up out of my bed. I can remember them carrying me back there, and I can remember them saying, "He has gone mad with the fever." Then I think that in the night I did go mad with the fever, for they told me afterwards that I howled and yelled and screamed for my sword to fight the gnomes and hobgoblins, and the things of hell and air; but, as I say, this I only learned long afterwards. I strove with death hard-handed, and I held him in my grasp, and he could not throw me; and at last the wrestle came to an end, for he slipped from me and disappeared, and I lay on the bed with wide-open eyes, my white face making the rough men who were in the room use words of which they were ashamed after, to me. Then came my wife, and her hand pulled the last of the fever from me; but the wrestle had left me very tired, and I lay many days knowing little. At last I could sit in the great chair by the window on sunny days, and look forth over the snows that covered my uplands and count the familiar trees which stuck up black out of the snow-drifts. Then they wrapped me in many coats, and with a man on each side of me I came down into the hall again, my wife behind me. It was the time of noonday meat, and the men rose with a hoarse shout as they saw me and pressed forward with outspread hands; but my Lady Elsa was before them in a moment, and her green robe shone strangely against their skin-clad bodies. She stopped them with gentle, firm words, asking them to let me get to the great chair that I might sit down, for I was come to eat a bite with them and drink a sup of ale; and the men sat down with a sigh, such as dogs give of contentment after full feeding. So I sat me down, and they brought me a tiny bird on a little plate and I could only eat half of it. Then they brought me a great tankard of ale, and I raised it to my lips and drank the half of it, and I felt the manhood rush to my feet, and then to my head again, and through my arms as I put the mug back on the table, and the men nodded to one another as saying, "It is well done for a sick man." Then slowly I finished the rest of the ale, then walked feebly to the fire and stood there warming myself. Then the two men who stood by me led me back to my chamber, and my wife followed, laying cool cloths on my head. Now every day I walked feebly to my meat in the hall, but it was not till the third day that I began to notice something strange about the men. They would look at me with a great curiosity, and some of them with seeming contempt, at which I said nothing; and one of the two men who had been my nurses in the sick chamber would follow me even through the gardens, as I walked slowly abroad with a staff for the keen frosty air; so that after some weeks I spoke to my lady about it, but she answered me, shaking her hair about her shoulders, that she knew not these western peasants as I did, and that in her father's hall there had been no suspicions and no glances of double meaning. Then spoke I to the man who followed me so faithfully as I have said, but he would answer nothing save that he thought that something was in the air, and that the spring would bring new flowers. Then asked I of young Heinrick, who still awaited the death of Father Cefron, with those laughing eyes under the wild light hair; but he laughed at me again, and told me that I was a sick man on one side of my head now and suspected everybody, and that I should send for a physician to plaster me — if he could find the side. Now old Father Cefron seemed to have dried into one of his own parchments, and his hide wrinkled, and almost rattled, as he walked. Though he came to eat with us in the hall on holy days, and said long prayers with somewhat worldly warnings after, yet he would on most days eat in his own chamber, and that of the least and coarsest, and would drink only of the ice-cold water from the well. I went to him at last and questioned him, and asked him if he had noticed the glances cast upon me, and the whispering and the sudden ceasing of the women's tongues when I came into the room, but he answered "No!" that he had noticed none of these things, for he was too much taken up in battles and kings and the histories of nations, to see aught that passed about him; and then he told me of the ancient days, and of the mighty, warm, strange, empires of the south and east, and spoke a hundred names of battles and knew every half-month of the history of the Church; and so I left him, comforted with learning, and went and sat and looked out on the snow, and thought of all that he had said.

The acts of the night that broke my life were short and quick, yet they are too long for the telling; still I will try, for without them you will not understand the strange end of this tale by the grey wolves.

It was the next night after this, and I had sat late in the hall, just beginning now to find strength enough to think of what I should do with my lands and cattle when the soft weather and springtime came at last. Sighing and putting these thoughts away from me as something too far off to be yet of use, I rose and through the darkened hall passed through the tapestried doorway and up the dimly-lighted stair, where the candles were distant, to my wife's room, before which hung a curtain that I had bought her in the Port of Swenborg from a ship that had come from the east countries, and as I raised the curtain in my hand, seeing by the faint light of one candle high on the wall behind me the great oak panels of her familiar door, I stopped. I stood still, the curtain in my hand, and the light flickered over the saints' heads carved on the oaken panels, and over my head. At the arch of the doorway stood an oak figure of a saint only the projecting edges of whose robe and face could be seen in the candle-light. I stood there while the candle blew and flamed; I heard its dripping on the floor; I glanced once toward the staircase, where the descending uncertain lights led down into the dusk and darkness. Somewhere in the distance outside the hall I heard a man singing in a coarse voice, then his comrades joined in the chorus, and I heard their "skaals." I stood there holding the curtain while the stairs creaked mysteriously as to the ears of a weary and sick man, and while, through the window near me, curtaining clouds flitted past the face of the moon as she looked down on the infinite purity of the untrod white below.

Then I dropped the curtain, and stealing down the stairs like a thief in my own house, I came again into the great hall, and I went and took down my sword from its place, and I sat me down in the great arm-chair piling the cushions around me, with my sword across the arms and my hands resting on its sheath. At last the dawn came faintly; then a long stain of yellow light struck across the ribbed and worn floor; then for a moment, a glorious red glowed through the windows, and then this faded and the ashes of the dead fire, and the broken meats that strewed the table, and the tankards that lay on the floor, sprang out under the truthful day. Then began to come in the women to carry out the things of last night, and when they saw me sitting there alone, they curtseyed and looked frightened and would have turned back, but I spoke to them quietly to clear the floor and build up the fire, for it was a cold morning and the men must have good meat; and after a while came in some ragged boys carrying bunches of branches and some hauling great bundles of logs with roots, and these they rolled into the fireplace piling the branches above them. Then one of the women, bringing a sack of dry leaves arranged them carefully among the branches and under the places where the bark of the logs was rough. Then, with a flint and steel, an old woman knelt and touched the dry leaves into a flame that was dull in a moment. The branches caught, and crackling, sent ends of flaming twigs wild up the chimney. Then at last the great logs at the back began to smoke, and soon their bark caught fire, and their chopped ends played with the eager flame, so all the hall was warmed and a thin smoke sailing up about the rafters. Then came they with great hooks that were made fast to turning cranes driven in the fireplace wall, and on these hooks were sides of deer and legs of sheep, with pans below and ladles that no richness might be lost, and thick brown cakes were piled along the table-centre in a row; and now four men came rolling in two casks of unbroached beer, and these they set below the table's edge down at the end. The women lifted a great cauldron on to the fire, that glowed like some sprites' cauldron of black-art; it held fowls and green things floating in the midst, the gravy sizzing at the sides. Then the old woman who had lit the fire went to the doorway and took down a great sea-shell that hung there and she blew a hateful blast that broke the very air, and all the men came trooping to their meat.

That morn was the holy morn of Easter, and Cefron came to share our meat, his elbow sideways over Heinrick's shoulder. My wife came later, and was blessed and sat. When Father Cefron had done his prayers, and given his pious warnings to the men, the food went from the table in a turn of the hand, for the morning was very cold and the men were hungry and the ale warm from the fire, where the men placed it. It flowed down thirsty throats like strong streams into caverns. When all had eaten and turned their stools apart from the board and leant their backs thereon or stretched their legs and arms in full content, I rose from my great chair at the head of all the table of my house, and with no word to her who was my wife, I pointed and I spoke to Heinrich quietly:

"You will meet me in holmgang, in the cleared snow, before the hall's great door, when the sun is even overhead, and you will fight me till you are dead, or I am dead."

He rose slowly to his feet, his face grew a dark red and his eyes seemed to go back under his brows in his anger. He said no word but stood there steadily looking at me. I seemed to feel his question how much I knew, and with one glance at Father Cefron's lifted claw-like hand, and one glance at the white face of Elsa, who was my wife, I answered in a low voice:

"I stood outside the door of Elsa, my wife, last night, after the moon had risen, and I held the curtain, and I listened to the voices, and I listened for a long time, and then I came away."

There was a sudden tearing of cloth, and a flutter behind me, and looking I saw Elsa, who was my wife, fall through the doorway which led from the banqueting-hall. Then young Heinrich turned the broadness of his back to me and stood a moment his right hand to his chin. Then he came to his place at the board again and sat down and began to eat; but as he raised the first mouthful of meat to his lips, he nodded to me, as to a horse-cleaner. I sat down and drank, for I would eat no more, while Father Cefron wept the tears of a very old man in a corner, laughing sometimes, and then raising his hand and seeming to curse us in laughing. The men sat silent with their brows drawn down. Only there was a smile on some of their faces when they looked at me— a heavy smile of kindness.

As the shades grew shorter and we could hear the sound of the swish of the brooms in the snow outside the door, Father Cefron regained his senses, and rising, and tottering toward me, and grasping each shoulder with a clutching hand, he tried to shake me, murmuring curses on the old gods meanwhile and sending them all to Hell in Latin and Danish. Then he began to blame me, and though he did not curse me as he had done the gods, yet he so poured out words that I had need to stop my ears to get away from their cold reasoning. Then he spoke for a long time on the hereafter, and told me the stories of the saints, and then he cursed the devil and his works, and then he prayed for me. Then rising, he commanded us both by name, his hands raised in the air and his white sleeves falling back from his bony forearms, to leave this holmgang or else we were cursed. He sank upon his knees and prayed to us, and then the shadow from a tall, gaunt tree that I was watching from the window touched its foot, and lifting my sword I turned to where young Heinrick sat, his deep brows wrinkled and his hair pulled down, and walked to where he stood. He did not move. I reached and touched him with my sheathed sword. Slowly he got up, and turning from me he went to the wall where his fair rapier hung. Then he came back to where I stood, and stopped. We stood so for a little while; then calling to one of the men who stood near, I cried hoarsely, "Touch him with the spit," and I could see the red of the back of his neck fail into whiteness as he went before me striding fast down the hall. I turned when we got to the doorway. Far away, by my great chair, knelt old Father Cefron, his head covered with the sleeves of his robe, and by the fireplace three or four women were crying with their faces in the corner.

It was a short holmgang. When we were ready I rushed him quickly, for I had my old heavy sword and his thing was light; but he sprang aside from me, and my sword whizzed past his shoulder. Then I turned and rushed him again, and again he sprang aside, his sword brushing my hair; and again I rushed him, and again he jumped aside, this time he struck me through the right forearm. So it went on till the shadows began to creep a little way from the trees, and I was very bloody and he had but one hurt; and then as I drew back to hit him, caring little for myself, his sword was through me, and I fell and kicked up the snow, then turned on my back. Then suddenly I was still and men pressed around me, saying, "He is dead"; but, I saw with my open eyes, Heinrick leap upon the ice-crust, and with his naked sword cutting the air as he ran in rage or wantonness, he fled, and was so far away that my men stood there staring. Then they carried me back to the banqueting-hall and through into my own chamber, and as we passed the kneeling figure of Father Cefron, I heard the men who carried me answer to the women by the fire, who whispered to them, "Dead on Easter morning, 'tis an awful day; but old men die, and so has Father Cefron—though he was a learned man."

Late that day the women came and washed me in my chamber and swathed me in white folds, and they pulled down my eyes so that I could not see, and they pushed up my jaws, but it seemed I needed not to breathe; and that night three women and a man sat with me all night, and the next night after that two women, and the next night after that one man, he who had followed me through the gardens before I had found about Elsa, who was my wife; and on the fourth morning, late after the sunrise, they lifted me and carried me forth upon their shoulders, a great white cloth with fringes hanging over me; and then I heard the tramp of many feet, and women crying, and the consoling tones of men, and I heard the pipe of children in the distance, and the crackling of the snow beneath the feet of the four men who bore me; and at last they laid me down upon the stones and they pulled down the cloth from my face and then I heard a voice speaking very low—the voice of Elsa, who had been my wife, "Peace be to thee where thou art"; and I tried to turn from the cold breath—for I could feel the cold as I could feel the warmth of that breath—but I could not, for my flesh was dead but my spirit lived within me. Then they carried me into some dank-smelling place; I knew they had to stoop, for I could hear their shoulders scrump along the passage, they laid me down on a shelf of stone and took the white thing quite away, and then they left me, and then I heard a sound of labouring at the door, and then a crash.

Slowly in the darkness I fell away, but

the life that runs through the body gathered itself away from the fallen parts, and when I was brown and thin my self burnt strong, and then I heard a note of freedom in the dark. It was like music, as my body went, and as my legs and arms became slim sticks, and as the years made my hands and feet not like human hands and feet, and as the inside of my body dried and fell; and one spring and summer passed and my spirit grew ever nearer its birth, I heard the soundless music breathing freedom night and day. At last my brain grew hard as my heart had grown years before, and all the parts of me decayed and shrivelled up until I was a brown, slim, wrinkled, hide that held some bones: no more. At last a great storm shook the place one night, and snow came in and wind and rain, and then my spirit was freed at last; for, sagging from its place, a rock fell inwards where I lay, and my brown bones were crushed and scattered.

Then I rose through the storm of the night, and I held to the tops of the trees, and I dropped and the water drenched me as it rushed past the banks of the streams, and I seized branches in the moonlight and threw them aloft and had joy to see the wind carry them. Then I came to myself again, and coming to the earth, tramped through the wood, to give me customs as live mortals have; for I was alive, having been killed, and though my body was dead and myself invisible but potent with hard grasp of hand, and flight in air, and strength of foot, I walked on the earth a thing that no God surely ever wished to make in his creation. I was a man with all a man's forces and all a man's heat, but I was as air to everything, and I held myself as I pleased. Soon I came to the old hall, and entering through the great door—for doors were nothing to me, yet I could open and shut them with my hands—I found the banqueting hall most desolate and only some few seats now near the fire; and passing on into the upper rooms I heard deep snoring coming from one of them, and looking in, I saw a young man that I did not know, who lay and slept beside a great wolf-dog. The wolf-dog turned and raised its head and howled, and I crept down the stairs again and out and on.

So all that night I journeyed toward the shore, and as the morning broke the far blue ice stretched before me and I travelled on. I travelled on over the ice-cakes, shoving on with my rusty sword where water was; and so from crack to crack and block to block, I crept until I was half-way across; then I sat down and laughed and nearly fell back into the water, for the ice-block tipped. I had forgotten that the air was mine, and that as the birds, or as the winged men and women that the priests have in pictures, I could go where I would; so I rose from the ice, and the wind sang across my rusty sword-hilt, and the air was keen, so that I opened wide my mouth and crossed the ice to land. So in three days I saw a great smoke rising, and a low stone hill that lay between the last snow and the bend of the sky. This I passed over in the night time, and the lights shone there for miles from the city and then I went on through the moonless night, until a great hall stood against the sea there. This I knew was Elsinore, and so I stopped and rested in a pack of straw that lay in a stable near the castle's rearward gate. The tempest howled around me and the straw whistled as if for fear, but I lay quiet, for all long cares had quite dropped away.

The next day and the next night too, I lay and rested there in a strange content that hurt me sometimes when I felt it most; but on the third night, having gained great strength, and ground my sword — when lights gleamed down from the castle windows and Elsinore was gay for some king's whim—I went across the moat and through the gates, and by the side-door of the castle to where a sleeping soldier stood, his lantern flaring. I entered into a long corridor, and passed down to a door that just shone at the other end. I opened it, and came into a small, gay room where three young pages sat, who cried out at the draught from the opened door: they did not see me, and I kept my sword away from them, though I remembered that, I being invisible, they could see as well on whichever side of me I held it. Then opened I the other door: at once the full lights blazed upon me, and the hum and sweet wail of dance-music came, with smell of flowers, and I wondered as the old flowers sent me their greetings if he was here, as I thought he would be. Then stealing through the room, through the dancers, I passed into a corner where sat some young tired men who looked like sleeping. He was not there. I passed between the dancers once again, and came into a corner where there sat some foreign-looking men with light-haired dames—bowing and paying them compliments, I think. I passed between the dancers then again, and passed before where sat the king and queen both weary-looking; yet with quick eyes, I could not find him. Then the music ceased and the dancers went back to their seats once more. Then passed I down the middle of the hall into the farthest corner, where there sat a group of ladies speaking in low voice, and men who leaned and talked and laughed and grinned, and as I passed through the crowd I saw the face of Him, and all the floor trembled. He sat back in the corner, very old: his long white hair fell on his sloping shoulders; his thin white hands were clasped upon his knees and his thin legs were thrust in velvet boots from which the fur stuck out. He had strange gold things on his chest and front, and a short beard that straggled round the chin, but his long hair fell over it; and every moment he would lean forward and mutter to the women near him some tale of woman's talk forgotten when half finished. I stood looking, in a corner where the stair ran up to the musician's gallery, I stood beneath the stair where I could see his face from out the shadow and where no one could see the sword, and there I stood and I hated him until there was a sound of rustling in the hall and of men's feet upon the smooth wood floor; and as I turned to look I saw the king and queen rise and go out, and then after a little time the others also went, and nearly last, he rose. A man had

Where the Wolves Dance

come to him from the pages' room and now held him under one arm as he tottered across the floor. I followed slowly, my old sword tight grasped. At last we reached the little gay-draped door. The pages' room was empty, and the corridors laughed to our heel taps as if mocking the dancers. And so we went out. There was a great chair there held by two men; into this he went; but I had my own mind of where to go so my old rusty sword was through the back of the hind chairman in a moment's time, and as he fell, the forward man ran round to try the door again, crying out; but I swung my sword and hit him in the side, and the old blade grided in so that the stuff came out, and he fell down dead on the steps. When the noise these men were making had stopped, I went and opened the door and sat me down inside with Him, and in a very few soft words told Him who I was; but being so old He could not understand though He was very frightened and knelt down trembling in the bottom of the chair. Then I asked Him where were horses, and He told me, mumbling, and I went to a farmer's stable and took a horse out, first feeding him well and giving him drink; then on this horse I put Him and wrapped Him in the horse-cleaner's old rugs and cloths. Then mounting up behind him, I guided the beast to the main road that runs along the water, and for many hours we travelled, jolting, in the darkness. Then the moon rose, and all the world was silver, and the sea lay black except where the sword-blade from the moon was laid across it. The moon was high. It was as light as day when I turned inland from the sea at last, and underneath great trees, and past small hills that rose and left dark hollows where drifts lay, we went. It was as light as the light of day, when all the hills seemed to rise up about us in their whiteness, and the trees stood black on the summits, white on their tops, and casting huge shadows that moved.

"Here," I said; and getting down from the horse, I turned to Him and lifted Him down also. "This is the place," I said; and taking Him under the arms as

Where the Wolves Dance

I had seen the serving-man do, I led Him down into the valley where the snow did not break to our tread, and standing there in the valley, holding Him under the arms, I called aloud three times the cry of a wolf. For a long time we stood there in silence till the cry had long echoed away; then from the right of me there slid a white wolf from the hill-top. He slid to the bottom of the hill a little way from me, and then sat on his haunches and looked at us with his red eyes. Then came three more wolves, slowly, over the snow; they came down from under the beech trees that were in front of us, and these also sat down on their haunches and stayed looking at us with their eyes. Then came one wolf more from in front of me, who did as the others had done. Then others came, till there were almost thirty of them, and they sat and stared at us; but whether they could see me I know not. The moon was just over us, and neither He nor the wolves cast any shadow. I turned and took Him in my arms, and holding Him to me, I whispered in a low voice, "You will fight holmgang here with me to-night." He did not understand, and His fine white hair lifted a little in the breeze. From above on the hill-top looked the horse that we had ridden, stupidly; I had tied him to a branch of beech, and the wolves sat round making no noise except the whispering and the brushing of their tails in the snow-glaze. I still held Him in my arms. "You will fight now," I said, "before the moon casts its shadow, and then I will leave You"; and he shuddered a little, and shook his head, this time half-understanding. I held Him close, pressing the horse-cleaner's cloths about Him. "You must take out your sword, and you must fight with me — you must fight with me here, now."

"Why?" He murmured feebly, His head sinking on my shoulder.

"Because I say it!" I answered in the same low voice; and with that I held Him from me and began to untie the cloths. When He was free, I drew myself apart and unsheathed my old sword, leaving the belt and scabbard lying on the snow by one of the wolves. Now I went up and whispered to the trembling figure again, "You shall fight!" I whispered, still in a low voice.

"I will not fight!" He said.

"You will fight for your honour!"

"I will not fight!" He replied.

"You will fight for your name."

"I will not fight," He said once again.

Then I stopped for a moment. Then I went up to Him slowly, and whispering to Him, "I was the husband of Elsa, and you broke my life when you were young, and now that you are old and I am dead, I shall kill you here where the wolves stand"; and with that, lightly, that I might not strike Him down, I hit Him on the cheek.

For an instant He stared at me, one side of His face white as the other grew crimson, and His old eyes flashed for a moment, and His shoulders squared themselves; but His arms, after one quick motion, hung still at His sides, and I heard Him murmur again, "I will not fight!" Then a wrath seized me, and swinging my sword on high I stepped slowly towards Him and let my point drop back slowly over my shoulder till it hung down to the snow, then wheeling suddenly and bringing it forward with a shortening of the arms and a yell that echoed through the empty forest, I hit Him with the rusty blade where the neck branches to go to the shoulder, and my blade travelled till it struck the hip-bone on the other side. Then with my foot on His waist, I drew my sword out and wiped it on the snow; wiping it many times till it was quite clean, then picking up the sheath and buckling the belt around me, I covered my sword and passed between two of the wolves and up the hill, and away to where the horse was tied. The moon fell down straight into the valley, and as I rode back again the way I had come under the dark trees and past the glittering hill-tops, I heard behind me melancholy howling coming from the place where the wolves danced.

This is all of my tale, except that I stabled the horse before dawn at the farmer's, and gave him food and drink, and then walked by the sea road as the dawn broke.

THE SACRILEGE

THE SACRILEGE

THE hall was raised at one end into a square stage, where the smoke would gather when the men sat late near the fire, and from this stage two doors opened at the back corners. One of these doors was curtained and led to the apartments of the men of the castle. The other was carved with strange images, and by it stood a long square table of carved oak. We men sat below at the long board which ran the length of the hall. It was my lord and the monks who lived upon us who sat upon the raised staging; the monks eating at their carved table apart.

It was after the dinner, and Father Peter rose in his place. Motioning to his followers to pass through the door that led to the chapel, he came and bent and whispered to my lord, who set down his beer-mug on the instant, frowning; then, after a moment's thought my lord lifted his hand and spoke to us all in a loud, clear voice:

"Father Peter and I would speak alone in the hall. It would please me that you men take your beer on the battlements."

The men went shuffling, all but myself, for I was my lord's own man and counted as nothing more than his follower, doing things which women usually do for men, for he would have no women-folk about him.

Now Father Peter, folding his fat hands across his chest, lowered his head and frowned reflectively. My lord sat silently in the great chair with one leg over the arm.

"Lord Rolf," said Father Peter at last.

"Yes, Father Peter," answered my lord.

"Lord Rolf, Christian of this castle," said Father Peter again.

"Ay! Christian, and certainly lord of this castle," answered my lord, smiling.

Father Peter raised his head, and lifting one arm, pointed at my lord.

"I have caused it that we should be

alone, that I might pray with you, for you are not so good a Christian as I would have you be."

"Yes," said my lord.

Then Father Peter, tumbling to his knees, prayed for a long time, while I standing by the fire, cursed his Latin. Then he got up again and coming to my lord he touched him on the shoulder.

"Have you felt that prayer?" he said in a deep voice.

"I have heard it," said my lord looking down.

"Then I will even say something that will appeal to you in a more militant way—something that has been in your mind for a long time, my lord." Father Peter became impressive. "The black frocks that sit and bend over that carved table by that carved door are a greater nation than ever the nation of Danmark will be, or any nation will be, until another nation of such frocks rouses itself against us; and so long as we shall hold the souls of men, and their hopes and fears of the hereafter, in our hands as a sword, so long shall we be more powerful than any sword forged by gnome or fairy."

Father Peter, extending both hands in blessing over Lord Rolf's head, turned hastily and went through the door that leads to the chapel. Now, this I would not stand, nor my lord, and we dared not tell it to the men for fear of violence, that the priests, who had forced themselves upon us in our house, and built their chapel leaning against our keep, should threaten us over the tables where they fed with us. This had been a long time coming, for Christianity sat hard upon us. There were no tortures in the time of Thor and Odin; and, as I said, Christianity sat grievously upon us.

Ah! Well! To the next scene. My lord was in the passage before Father Peter's room, and he knew that Father Peter would return alone from the chapel after his last devotions, and when Father Peter's dark bulk turned the corner of the oak stair my lord spoke to him out of the shadow.

"Father Peter, you have said some

words to me to-night in my hall. They were not churchmen's words."

Father Peter hesitated a moment, then throwing back his head:

"No," he said; "they were words militant, for the Church is born militant; and she shall ride you as a plough-horse. Let me pass on from my devotions."

"No, Father Peter," said my lord in a quiet voice, reaching one arm out of the shadow. "You go where you have taught us that there is more devotion than there is upon this earth. For three years you and your crew have eaten, slept, and builded on my lands, until now my house is but very little my own."

Father Peter took a step forward, but the long white arm barred him across his thick throat. He strode one step farther forward, pushing the arm aside, and, turning in the direction of my lord's voice, snarled like a dog, calling him long names from books I never read. Whether my lord was mad, or whether the humiliation of the past three years had hurt his heart, I do not know, but he reached both arms around the priest, and lifting him in the air, flung him face-downward against the window, where it ran to the floor. I went to my lord and caught his hands behind him. Then drawing long breaths, we walked silently toward the black form at the window foot. Stooping, I put my hand over its mouth and over its fat chest. There was a drawing up of legs and something like a laugh, deep in the throat. Then Father Peter died.

. . . .

The snow chunked under our weary feet and our staffs were useless in the thaw, and ever behind, when the wind was still, and when there were no pines near us to whisper as of safety, we could hear the sound of the horses, and we would look at each other and step higher, and take longer strides for a few yards. My lord was very weary, for he was a man who loved warmth, and he could not bear the cold of the indifferent sky above him and the unfeeling purity of the snow that lay about us.

Far away was the glimmer of sea. There was no dawn, but a streak of yellow in the east, that grew and lengthened and widened, and then became flame-coloured and then disappeared, and a little sun came from the sea, but it had no light and the snow had glimmered more under the moon. There were but two of us left. We had been seven at first, but of the others three had turned back and two lay in the snow on our way. It was the ninth day that we had left the hall; and ever the men of the Bishop of Lund, three hundred and fifty of them, came after us on their light horses, and ever we doubled and crouched over the snow, like hares hungered or hunted. At night we would make fires of the pine-cones, and in our helmets melt the snow into water, lowering our helmets into the snow again to cool them afterwards. We had eaten all our bread, but of fish we had plenty, though I was sorry for my lord. So all that day we hastened, and when the night came we lay back to back in a hollow of the snow on a little hill that looked over a bay. The bay was frozen, and I remember the winter moonlight kept me awake as it shed itself upward from the ice into my face; and whenever I looked out over the snow-sweep, its long white track seemed to point to where we lay. Deep into the night, when the sighing wind had ceased to scud the drift-snow into our hiding-place, my lord turned over and shook me feebly. "Man!" he said; "he was right when he said the Church was born militant, and that only a greater power like itself shall cast a shadow on men. We broken clans, that call ourselves nations, are little things. What shall I do? Tell me, what shall I do?" I looked at him in the surprise of one just waking, as he knelt above me, one hand on each shoulder. "Man!" he said, again, shaking me, "what shall I do? They are coming; I can hear them under the snow. I can hear the ice of the bay cracking to their boats, and I can hear the whispered warnings of the pine trees when they bend to the stirred air of their innumerable breaths. Man! what shall I do?" Awake now, I saw that my lord was full of terror, like a child, and bringing him close to me, I rolled him in his clothes and put him deep in the snow again, piling some of my own things over him, and he slept complainingly and fitfully like a child who has been punished.

It was just before the dawn when we heard the far-away shouting of the Bishop's noisy troop, and crawling to our feet we left our hole in the snow and crept down the side of the hill toward the water. Here my lord thought it was easier walking on the ice, but soon we heard the sound of horses on the strand, and as it was a road to them not like the snow above, we climbed again to where the deeper drifts were and passed unseen. So half that day we travelled, and twice they went ahead of us going by the strand, but both times a few horsemen only; so we dared not turn back, for we knew the others were spread out on the uplands. Late in the afternoon we came to the long point of rock that stretches from our island towards the mainland, and here my lord stopped. "If we had a boat," he said, trembling I think with eagerness; then, pulling his grey beard, he whispered to himself only, "Who can fight against the Church,—who will not fight?" Then turned he again and went on along the shore; and thus late in the evening we came to a solitary beech which rose from out a hollow in the hills. Great formless mounds of white lay near, the fallen ones who had left this old tree lonely; and leaning against this solitary trunk we passed our night, until the coming of a glorious dawning fell on our faces as they lay against the smooth beech-bark, and awakened us early—I think earlier than any of the Bishop's men awakened that morning, for though we waited to eat we heard no sound of their pursuing until nearly the noon-time; then from far off came the familiar thud of horses' hoofs and the crisp jingle of the bridle-reins, in the far-carrying, cold, morning air.

It was the next day after this, when my Lord Rolf seemed to hesitate, walking by himself, telling even me nothing, and when it came to the sunset and a cold yellow edged the dark sky over the sea, and the snow-drifts looked ghostly at any distance, he spoke to me after many trials with himself.

The Sacrilege

"Do you know where we are?"

"No," I said.

"Do you know that by to-morrow at noon we shall have returned?"

I looked at him startled.

"Returned to the hall?"

"Yes," he said; "we shall have been round the island."

"And when we shall have returned?" I asked.

My lord was silent. It was not at noon the next day but toward the dusk when the darkening trees began to seem familiar, and the coast-line stretched in remembered curves, and the ripples along the icy beach seemed home-like. In the dusk, as we plodded crouching behind a drift of snow that ran along the hillside, there rose before us something gaunt and white and very tall and very still in the valley below us, and we stopped, for we saw it was a building: it seemed a keep of the old days that they build no more now. So we stood looking, trying to make out any light near in the dark evening. Suddenly my lord sighed, and, falling forward on his knees, he put his face down in the snow, and when I bent and whispered to him he only answered, "They have burnt it, but the old keep would not burn." It was our own hall that we had come back to. So, the next morning we struck inland again, from the hill-top, thinking to find refuge in a forest of leafless oaks whose rattling branches glittered in the pale sunlight; and when we reached it my lord sat down on a great root of one of the trees and would go no farther into the forest. So I stayed by him all day feeding him on the last of our fish, and making him cold water to drink, for though he shivered very much he drank always. Thus it was that midway between the noon and the evening there came three men, cross-bowmen, suddenly, from over the hillside, and seeing us they stopped; then after a moment's speaking one with another they ran forward, their cross-bows stretched.

My lord was sitting dejectedly at the foot of the ice-sheaved oak, and I was cooling water for him in my helmet.

The three men ran toward us, shouting. My lord heard the sound and looked up; then rising slowly to his feet, he hesitated a moment and unbuckled his sword, at which the three cross-bowmen stopped, for they were not great men. Then my lord spoke to me, half turning: "You have followed me faithfully, though to a bad end, and I can give you nothing; nor do you want it; but I will not be killed by Bishop's men. My fathers knew how to die, and their Gods took them, so I—— and my Gods will take me." Then ramming the hilt and the upper part of his sword into the snow, my lord fell over it awkwardly and lay groaning, the sword through him. All this before I could do aught but cry out.

Well—— Then came the bowmen, who shot him so that, after a few minutes, he was dead indeed, and they brought his body and his sword down to the snow-covered keep in the valley, where they delivered it to the Bishop of Lund's legate; and they showed me over the doorway the heads of many old women whom they said had been "left behind."

I do not know. And there were children's heads hanging from them. What became of the men of the hall? It is something that I cannot remember. They bound thongs of leather round my brows to make me tell of Father Peter and how he died, and again in Roskilde, and they twisted them. But at last they permitted me to enter the church here, as a server, and I look out on the fair fiord of Roskilde now.

I am very glad that the story is done.

THE
STORY OF THE OAR-CAPTAIN

THE STORY OF THE OAR-CAPTAIN

This is the story of the Oar-Captain, that they used to tell to harps; and that, after, was made a saga of. The story is rough, like the natures of men, and full of storm of Nature and sea, as if a fury had run down the pages. But there are soft threads in its rough woof—I tell it just as the Oar-Captain told it.

The sun sank over the right-hand side of the ship—red, while the sky was cloudless. And the light breeze fell, just as the dusk came, and our brown sail trembled for a moment, and then sank back against the mast. The men, laughing, leaned in a row along the bulwarks, while my lord paced up and down on the aft-deck. The steersman pulls in his oar, the ship swings idle, and soon the blue smoke ascends in a straight, fine line through the evening air from the open dish of black charcoal where they cook at the mast-foot.

It is evening, and soft clothes are spread about on the deck. Far away the sea stretches, till it fades into the glow of the almost dark sky; while on the other side, where no man looks, is dusk-darkness, cold, abandoned, the dead regions of what was morning. After a while, when the glory has quite faded out of the sky, the men murmur and slowly lie down on their clothes talking for a while. That gradually ceases, and we lie silent, while there comes faint creaking of cordage as the ship lazily swings. My lord has ceased pacing the aft-deck. We lie watching the stars come out.

Slowly they come, the eyes of other worlds. Lying close under the rail I see a little track of lights come from far away, till it seems they become scared and stop, and other lights come out behind them—a twinkling row, till they reach the bulwark over my head. Next me a man sighs in his sleep.

I lie thinking of the lands to the south,

and of my lord. When I turn my head I can still see him in the gathering dark, where he leans dim by the black line of the steering-oar. Looking up my soul leaves the ship, and seeming to gaze down from the stars I feel very far away. Slowly they come, silent lights. I remember old sagas and faces—old faces——

It is morning. The fresh wind lifts the sail outward; the hair is blown in the men's faces; the water whispers and chuckles merrily under the side of the leaning ship. The thin ropes creak, the shields over the sides rattle and jerk. I and another swing on the steering-oar, and the men run along the decks with glad faces.

It is afternoon. The ship lies on her side; the flying water runs over as it goes by. Dark clouds have come out of the east, and are streaked from their low-lying bank in long streamers along the sky. The mast bends, the bows shoot the spray up into the winds, where it is whirled away before us. The water hisses; the wind moans and sings; and the ship is full of the rattle of the oars along the benches.

It is evening. The moving sky is as black as the water between the foam-streaks, by which we rush; through a vapour-veiled hole, dimly, the pale sun is going down. Men shout to each other in the dark, and the water splashes in waves along the benches. My lord gives orders for the sail to be rolled fast and that all men shall come off the fore-deck.

Morning. By the hazy light from far up in the heavens, I see our bare mast with the tangled bunch of ropes whipping forward from the top.

Broken oars swim in the water in the waist of the ship, and from outside, heard in the twilight, comes the sound of mermaids singing I think, answered by the dull roar of the mermen's shells. I look around; before me are the men holding to anything that is firm on the after-deck, where my lord stands, looking forward. They are pale, and the glistening of their clothes shows in the misty light, that shows the foam hissing over the side of the ship.

So, all day we crouch, gnawing pieces

Story of the Oar-Captain

of bran-bread, and holding fast to the sides of the ship.

Evening. The sun has gone out, and a roaring that sounds like the rushing of pine-trees falling, comes from the dark. The shields are gone, and the men laugh grimly thinking of death, when the seas rush over the flying bulwarks.

It is morning again, and the clouds rolling and flying in jagged flags in the wind, are broken at sunrise, and the wind sings now, not roars.

The ship shows, a bare-sided, dripping, unfamiliar thing beneath the morning light; full of wreckage and ropes, the sail lying, and the yard gone, the bunch of ropes at the top of the mast. The pale men that have ceased to laugh now, untie themselves from the bulwarks and creep stiffly forward to the food-chest. The sea rises in waves, but the still stiff breeze keeps them down and we ride on, plunging; our bare mast shakes in the wind.

That is how, when Lord Uffē stood on the seaweed-brown beach four days later, he was cried to over the side of a bare-masted ship as it rowed round the point along the rocky shore, and asked the name of the country.

Lord Uffë brought us up to the hall where his people ran to cook meat for us, and where we sat gladfully drinking the warm ale by the fire. Then the great platters of meat came in seething, and we sat and ate, warming ourselves, while Lord Uffë talked to my lord at the end of the table — sitting by a great red-haired man that he ever glanced at kindly, but who with thoughtful eyes sat gazing as one seeing nothing.

As we sat there, when our first hunger was done and men were beginning to stretch out their legs under the table, I looked about the hall. And there was something that seemed strange about it. For some time gazing, I could not see; then with a half-afraid feeling, a wonder, I saw that everything was old — the benches, the arms rusted on the walls — it was as if men had been dropped back three centuries. Even while I was yet wondering at this and looking curiously at the old-patterned arms on the walls — such as I had seen in the old halls we had stopped at in our sailing, kept from ancestors — the lord of the place, Lord Uffē — a short, stout, strong, old man, with kind face and a beard to his waist and eyes that shut in his laughter—rose, and standing with his hand on my lord's shoulder, spoke to him and to the table so that all might hear.

"Ye care to know," he said, smiling, "what country this may be. Then I will tell a story to you all — see that ye are comfortable—

"Four men's lifetimes ago if they were old men there was a ship blown off the coast while it bore a boat-load towards the south, from a burnt town in the hard north; searchers for new places. And for days a great wind blew them the same as it has blown you, till, in the night, no moon, they fell upon this place, the ship shocking onto the sands and falling in pieces, and some of the men killed. They sat in the hiding of the rocks till the sunrise, then with the strong wind blowing in their faces, they found their home, built it, and saved some things from out of the ship—they were my fathers. A pleasant country; we are content; no ships ever come; we are alone; we mow our easily-sown fields while our children grow about us; we cut timber in limitless forests—why should we leave it? The name of the place?" And he stood, his great beard falling on his chest, his eyes looking kind along the board to see if we wanted anything.

"We are lost in the seas," he said again. "Whether far or near, or north or south, no man knows; no ship ever comes; the forest begins behind us; nothing that shows sign of man's hand is washed to the shore; we are alone, lost and contented. Listen to the sound of the sea; we have never crossed it; no man has crossed it to us; we know not where it goes; or where we are."

The old man spoke grandly, but his kind eyes ever glanced along the table to see if we wanted anything.

We men drew long breaths, and I saw my lord draw down his brows, and tug the fair hair over his forehead. Some of us got up, and began to walk about.

Then in the midst of the silence my lord spoke hesitatingly.

"We thank my Lord Uffë for his kindness. What can we do—can we sail home—and where? Still, for the present, we thank my Lord Uffë for his kindness."

The old man, pulling his beard, stood, looking at my lord for a moment; then, a smile coming to his lips and showing in his eyes, he held out his hand and said, "Stay."

It was some days before we got the things out of the ship and the ship well hauled up on the beach. Then we looked about for a place for our houses; for we had decided to stay, at least for a while.

The land seemed good; the sand, broken with rocky points, stretched straight along the bright sea; and, protected from the sea-winds and storms by a line of oak forest left standing, lay fields now just green in the spring-time. Beyond these fields, fenced off from one another by little walls of stone, drew in the forest again, the colour of the light-green of a curling wave, and as limitless as the sea. In the edge of the forest, surrounded by a few of the great trees, the others being taken away, on a little rise in the ground, stood the old wooden hall of Lord Uffē, shaded by the green branches, or crossed by the patches of sunlight when they waved — the hall, a low building, old, with many passages inside and far-away little rooms, and the one great dining-chamber; built very stoutly. Around, in the edge of the forest, were little houses of wood from which the smoke curled lazily up in the spring air, and about which ran children playing while their happy-faced mothers watched from the doorways. The sky was very blue, birds sang in the trees, and about the fields hopped little hares.

We decided to build our hall, not a large one, but enough for us, farther down the row of fields in a little point of great old trees that ran out a little way toward the cleared place. Here with our axes we hewed for many days, cutting great timbers and raising them upright along the sides of our house-

Story of the Oar-Captain

floor. Then came dragging of logs through the forest and the laying them one on the other along the timbers for the walls of the house and the driving of wooden pins and hewing of doorways.

All this time we lived at the hall of Lord Uffë, except some of us who stayed in the houses round.

I lived at the hall. Thus I saw from the beginning, the trouble that came to us, and that brought storm and madness. Here, lost from all men, with the unknown sea between us and all things but the birds and woods and trees and waters and our little selves, was played a thing that was unchanged from the far places we had left, as though we had never left them.

While the fields grew greener, and the birds sang, and our house was growing nearer finishing, while Lord Uffë walked in the forest and our ship lay on the beach and our men ate in the hall, my lord, with his yellow hair, and his soft harping, made love to the daughter of Lord Uffë's dead brother, the betrothed of the friend of Lord Uffē, the great man who had sat in the hall silently when we found welcome there.

It was this way. One day, when the noon held all the fields in stillness and the little singing things were silent in the grass, I walked—for the day was too warm to work in the mid-day—slowly, along one of the forest paths, just shut off from the glare of the sun in the open by a screen of trees whose leaves hung still in the silence. Then, far before me, I saw at the end of the path two figures, and stopped, I do not know why. I saw who the figures were — my own lord and Hilda, the betrothed of his friend.

They were coming toward me, but their heads were bent down, and they did not yet see me. I waited; though they walked slowly it seemed but a moment till they were close to me; they were walking in silence. I know not why, but I turned softly and went back, they not seeing me. As I went back the silence oppressed me and I wanted the sound of the crickets in the grass.

Story of the Oar-Captain

When I came into the hall that night for my meat, and looked up at the end of the table where she sat by the great man, I sat down in the shadow and was ashamed, for I saw it all.

Perhaps it was that we were new and strange, or perhaps it was my lord's harping, and songs, and gentle ways, that took the maiden's liking—she to whom the world was a legend. The people about her were rough; she, in her simple dress, had learnt from the delicate flowers and things of the woods where she had lived, to find them so perhaps. But when I looked up from the shadow and caught the gleam of my lord's eyes as they met hers, looking across the forms of Lord Uffē who had welcomed us, and her betrothed, in this old hall; where below, sat our men and Lord Uffē's together, all their hands hard from the work on great timbers—I grew sick.

I have no heart for this part of the tale; let me go on to the ending.

For many days I stayed by our unfinished hall where the men were busy thatching the roof and making the fireplace and windows; it was almost done. At last one night I trod wearily up for my meat at Lord Uffe's, while the air felt heavy and the occasional thunder that had rumbled far away all day, growled in the west, as the sun sank. I came into the hall when they were all seated, and without looking up at the end of the table sat myself down silent, while the man next to me growled like the thunder as he shoved me the meat-dish.

After dinner they called on my lord for a song. He took down his harp from where it hung on the back of his chair, and striking it three times—I remember all these small things—bent his head for a moment as if listening. Then turning, and facing down the hall, he lifts his head; and, playing softly, his voice rings out in a love song, that brings the tears into the eyes of the women by the fire in a moment. As it rises, it wakes even us men—what was that? Only thunder. The song goes on. It speaks of love and despair, softly, but with a strange tenderness in the notes that makes each man apply it to himself.

Story of the Oar-Captain

The sorrowful notes droop through the hall to the running music of the strings—he turns toward the figure in white behind him—What a roar of thunder!—the song goes on.

It speaks of division and of sorrow, and love unknown; it speaks of the tenderness of love that is hid, of longing. A crash and volley of thunder just overhead, and the hall is lit up for a moment by the lightning—it is gone and the fire shines out again.

My lord is standing facing her; he leans forward, his eyes on hers, and plays softly, his voice falling low. We bend forward to listen. He is singing of love and its fulfilment; he sings of love, and the tenderness of it. Slowly the words fall, his head is bent forward and his eyes gaze into hers. Slowly she rises from her place, slowly she comes toward him, her head raised, her eyes on his, slowly she sinks at his feet—the notes fall—low——

Crash and roar! and a dying-away of the tumult into a distant roll while the hall is lit up for a moment by the lightning. The light flickers on the walls, showing the still raised harp, the kneeling figure, the men half-risen from their places. It is gone, and the fire that has died down glows feebly.

As I awake from the waking sleep I hear voices raised angrily, and in the dusk see two figures, one tall, risen by the bench at the end of the table. Someone throws a log on the smouldering fire and the sparks fly up. In a moment it is light.

I hear a voice shouting, "Dost thou love this man?"

And Lord Uffē's voice raised in remonstrance; and from the white figure now standing leaning against my lord comes a low voice saying something we cannot hear.

Then there is more tumult that gradually thins down to a single voice speaking, and Lord Uffē's words are heard as the silence falls. "Before thou cam'st we were content; but thou hast brought the noises of the world with thee, and broken peace. Thou cam'st to us out of the storm; go back into the storm, my guest!"

Story of the Oar-Captain

Slowly my lord went down the hall, we behind him. Turning my head—I was the only man who turned—I saw the white figure on its knees again by the bench, its head hidden. Our host stood, his hand out towards us; away by the fireplace a face shone over a huge black form on whose hair the firelight played. I wish I could forget that face!

As we passed in silence through the door the thunder roared and died away.

Soon we were at the ship in the darkness; we shoved her off in the darkness; we men hoisted the mended sail in the darkness; we heard the water begin to sound under our sides, then—a faint roll of thunder from far away, a long flicker of light across the sky. We saw my lord standing alone on the hind-deck, the beach, the lights of the hall—the lightning gone, and we heard the water rushing around our bow in the darkness.

Not a drop of rain fell; the air was very still.

When the day broke pink over the far level waters, my lord was leaning on the rail yet. As the yellow light reached over the water till it touched our ship I saw his face, and it surprised me, being quite gay. I went up to him, and, the men gazing silently at us, spoke to him.

"The men," I said, "will carry you home, or east, but then——" I stopped, for there was something in his face that made me stop.

"Yes," he said.

"And then we will leave you. If you wish, you can get a new crew."

"Ah," he said.

"I do not know how many days—when——"

"Yes," he said.

I stood silent; in the silence again; "Yes," he said, smiling to himself as if in fun.

I moved myself so as to get a look at his face. There seemed a horror in the eyes, and a stopping of all hope, that made me uncomfortable.

Waiting for a little time, I said again:

"If we come home——"

He did not answer. I was angry with him, and stood one foot uncomfortably over the other for a little while, and then went back to the men.

"He will answer only 'Yes,'" I said angrily. The men grunted, and I sat down, angry, yet not quite understanding, leaving him still smiling.

All day I sat, angry, and when evening came and we had eaten, grumbling, and cursing—all save my lord, who had eaten nothing—I got up and clambered again on to the hind-deck.

When I came to him I stood, all the words having left me. I seized my courage hard and spoke.

"When we get back, if we ever do, the men will leave you."

I waited; he gave no answer. I started to speak again, but no words would come. I tried again. Then, with a sudden movement I leaned round on the bulwark and saw his face. For a moment yet I stood impatient; then with a cry of rage and pity I seized his hand and held it a moment, then dropped it and rushed back among the men, and hid my face in a dark corner, and sat there cursing weakly in a childish feeling of impotency — oh, the shame; and the great woe he carried in his smiling face!

Toward evening the wind fell, and as the sun went down the water shone smooth, and the light blazed in our faces. The cool of the dusk was a relief, and long after the great red moon had risen, we lay, restlessly, surely a strange ship-load, lost on the limitless seas.

When morning came we pushed out our oars and toiled regularly, creakingly, over the level water. The sun blistered the wood of the bulwarks and burned our faces, and we longed for evening. So for twelve days; till the yard was crooked, and our faces the colour of tanned skin. The men used to groan at the oars. On the twelfth day, midway between sunset and dark, came a little breeze over the water, that made the men shout. And for two days we went unsteadily eastward and northward with the little puffs of wind.

All this time we saw no land and no streak of foam upon the sea, that was the colour of wood-ashes; only brown sea-weed drifting northwards. My lord had become very brown, and had a way of always turning toward the light, looking east when the sun rose and west when it set.

Now, for some days we went northward; then for more days we went east, till one morning, just after sunrise, we saw land, black hills which we had come near to during the night. And for two days we coasted along the great cliffs where the water beat white at their black bases. Then we came to some houses, then to a curve and dying down of the cliffs. Then a great wind took us and we were blown in, and all the rest was storm. Once we drove past a sandy desolate point of land that was gone in an instant; and once the ship grew almost full of water which we baled out in the darkness.

On the second night, as we were flying through the half-dusk — the moon shone sometimes — we heard a deep rushing before us just a little louder than the sea's rushing. In a moment there grew up in the darkness a shore of

waving trees—we were among rushes—
the ship high on the ground. We were
splashing ashore in the dark and the
swishing wind, and we sat and listened
under the tossing, complaining trees till
daylight.

Two days' travelling under darkly-dripping branches brought us to a hall. It looked familiar—it was our own hall!

We had come home!

How quickly wonders fade under joy, though sorrow preserves them long. By that evening we had come to think of it as very natural.

Three days we passed in eating and drinking, and on the evening of the third one we sat pale from our drinking along the board. Outside the ship lay, having been brought round by those sent.

My lord sat on a low stool by the corner of the fire. The talking grew slack and we yawned, the edge of our home-coming having been ground down by welcoming. Some of us rose to go to our sleep.

Then my lord stirred, uneasily, for a

moment, got up, walked slowly to the end of the long room, and sat down. We glanced around at the sound of his tread and then the little talking ceased, for we saw that he meant to speak. After a moment he spoke.

"I will go there to-morrow, and I would know what men would accompany me." His lips were tight closed and he was pale across the forehead.

No one spoke.

"Will no one go?" he asked softly.

After a moment, I said, "Where?" all the men frowning.

"To where we have come from, across the water," he answered, pressing his lips together till he showed white round the mouth.

The men sat, perfectly silent.

He came slowly to his feet, stopped, and then began to speak, softly and strangely, with a great kindness.

"Ye do not ask it, but though I believe ye do not even want it, I will speak in justification. I would tell ye a few things. In that far place she had seen but few men, only woods and trees and natural things. The man to whom she was betrothed not against her will—I will be fair — was little more than these to her in that dreamy place. Slow and dull, he had nothing to answer in her own-taught beauty. When we came, she did love me, truly, but in her kindness, she would stay his wife. She had Freya's soul. Her father's brother liked me. Thus things were when the night came of our leaving.

"One more—I had never asked her to be not true to her betrothed, so, I was dreaming, my soul drawn all one way.

"That night when I sang her the love-song—oh ye men of my house, have ye never done wrong? Are ye sure that the souls within ye would stand firm while they were pulled with mighty cables? Have ye never had an evil thought? Have your spirits always been level within ye? Can ye never be mad, and rock to the torment of it? Do ye understand?

"Well, the music went out of my harp, and tore me—Are ye stone walls, that ye would not have shaken down like the leaves of trees? I could have wailed like a child for its mother, or, like a hammer on beams, crushed a man's head with my hand.

"Are ye more than are men? Have ye never done any ill? I say, I stood there, dreaming, playing; my soul drew her to me; I stood there playing the old love-song, in agony. Then there was a noise of voices, and we went to the ship, and were many days coming home, being becalmed."

He stared straight before him — a wakening came into his face — he on a sudden raised his hands in the air, and, the shaking fingers widespread, called through the hall in a strange voice. "Oh great Gods, come!"

We sat silent in the lit hall, and the call died away into silence.

"Shame!" cried a woman's voice; "ye are not men!"

We stirred not even at this reproof from a woman.

"I will go!" cried the voice again, and one of the women who helped in the cooking stood forward with her great ladle held like a sword.

"Ay, and leave the ladle for the men to manage!" cried a second, a bare-armed, laughing woman, ranging herself by the other one, and turning a saucy face on my lord.

"Will ye lend us your swords, stay-at-homes?" called a third from beside the fire.

"We need not your help to shove the ship off the beach," said a young girl, haughtily, as she swept forward to the others and looked up at my lord from her little height.

There was stillness in the hall, while the three women stood looking up at my lord. Then some of the men got up, and frowning, hesitated, and then said they would go. Six of them. We others sat silent. The women fell laughing and pointing at us, and the lights flared merrily.

The next morning we watched the ship hauled down the beach and put out. And when she passed round the trees going by the shore, we lost her suddenly.

For months we waited—for a year.

She did not come back. Did they find the hall lost beyond the waters? Did my lord marry the maiden? Or were they drowned or lost?

I an old man write this now in "justification," as my lord said.

THE LAST VOYAGE

K

THE LAST VOYAGE

The ceiling was broken through in the corner over our heads, and clean-tongued splinters pointed downward; the big room was smoky from the roaring fire, and the table was covered with bottles; around sat some forty men. We were in our armour, except our head-pieces, for we had ravaged the country round, and had killed or driven away all living things. All but one; for the old woman of the house stood even now grinning in the corner. Round the walls were piled plate and beautiful armour, such as we had never seen before, and there were gold crosses and gold pots and chains; yet the men grumbled, till at last one threw his little cup into the fire and strode heavily to the door. He kicked it and it tumbled outward on one leathern hinge. The rest of us looked lazily up. A brown expanse of burnt vinelands, and in the distance a broken-roofed church and the black walls and chimneys of a few cottages that looked ugly and lonely and pitiful against the blue depth of the sky. The thought came into the minds of all of us I think, to leave this brown path that we had trod free of grass, for our ship lay only one day's march somewhere westward, and the half of our number again cursed the lots that they had drawn as they waited; but the old woman, who always grinned, poured yellow wine into our cups and took the old ones away, and we drank, and it made us courageous, so that we spent the evening wrestling by the firelight.

It was just before sunrise that I stirred sleepily and raised myself on my hands and knees. In a moment I heard clank and clash coming from the darkness all around me, then silence, but my mind saw grey things that crept in nearing circles. Ay, grey as sleep, around the house. As I woke my companions shaking them by their sword-belts, there broke out on the stillness of the night a loon's cry, from beyond some bushes by a narrow pond. We were lying outside under the overhanging front roof of the inn. We crept through the door, our swords in our hands, and each man hastily buckled on his armour. When we were ready we turned. Before the fire stood some twelve mail-clad men, with curious helmets and coverings for their elbows, and their swords were long, reaching from their shoulders to the floor. We stood looking each other in the face for a long time, then we backed slowly to the door and out of it, still gazing at them, into the pale uncertain light of the watery dawn, leaving them standing there in front of the glowing embers. We stole toward the narrow path in the growing light, and waited there in the bushes for sound from the house, our crossbows strung. At last, as we waited and watched, a crouching figure ran hastily round the corner of the house to the doorway. After this we waited for a very long time till the east was all gold, then suddenly a file of men, in plate to the waist, with long bows in their hands, stepped forth from the bushes on either side of the door.

Men who had grown up on these ravaged vinelands, and who had come from nowhere on vengeance they were; and as they grouped themselves around the corner of the house a sudden flare of red came through the doorway, and we could hear the crackling of lit wood from inside. Then there were shouts from our men in the upper chambers, and we heard their steel shoes on the stone stairway. There came the clank of steel on steel, and the steps on the stairway ceased. Now the smoke came from the windows in the upper chamber, and in a moment we heard a great rush across the upper floor —a rush that ended in falling bodies, and yells, and the breaking of wood, and three of our men broke through the doorway. In a moment they were down, each man with a goose-shaft in him. The bowmen closed in the doorway, and the house was filled with a roaring as of bulls, and the clanking as of a thousand anvils in caves; and the flames poured from the chimney. Now came the old woman who always grinned, rushing out through the doorway, but as she came, one of the men-at-arms who stood behind the others raised his bow, and she fell kicking over the pot-helm of one of our men. Last, came six more of our men, their clothes singed off outside their armour, and their faces deep red. They came through the door sideways, their sweaty swords turning in their hands as they struck, but in a moment they fell also, two by two; and then the tumult within the house died down, but the flames roared through the crumbling rafters, and the burning wisps of thatch lit up the distant poplar tops where the wide road curved in the distance. So we crept away over the burnt fields, crouching in ditches, with our swords drawn; we had no water all day, but we passed many cottages where no one came to the doors to stare at us nor smoke rose from the chimneys, and there was no waving of yellow grain on the hill-tops. We passed the bones of a horse, and after, part of the armour of a man— rough armour—and as the sun sank we passed a woman's head-covering lying dirty by the road. It was after the dusk, which comes stealing in these countries,

and blinds you from behind, sudden and
soft, that we smelt the sea, and we
stumbled forward hastily over a charred
hillside. The ground grew softer as we
descended, though now we could see
nothing. Soon we were on level, and
our feet sunk in the sand, and we heard
a rustle and a whispering just before us.
We ran forward and waded to our
waists in the unseen water. Ah! 'twas
good. Then we crept back to the hillside
again, where we lay until morning in a
hollow, covered with dead leaves; and in
the morning we were awakened before
the sunrise, by the strong salt wind in our
faces, and the lashing of what last night
had been dainty with playfulness. The
beach was brown with seaweed cast up,
and the spume of the light waves that
broke on the shore retreated in streamers and circles far out from the land
again. The keen wind whistled on the
edges of our armour and sang round
us, and we turned our faces from
it, and it blew our long hair into our
eyes, stinging us. Now, we knew that
the ship lay somewhat to the north of

us, for our lord had said that she should not pass a certain great rock, round whose top many gulls circled, but stay to the northward; so we tramped the heavy sands the gathering wind at our backs, and we stumbled over the piles of slippery seaweed and passed round the promontory, where was the Gull Rock. So it came to late in the afternoon and we were very weary, having had no meat or drink. Yet we kept on in silence, bending as we pulled our heavy feet from the sucking sand-holes. The spume blew in our faces now when the waves broke; the beach was narrow, and to our right were rocks which rose up straight into the air. So, as I say, it came to late in the afternoon. We were walking, each man in the other's footsteps, and I, being the largest and having the largest feet, went first. Suddenly I heard a sharp sound from one of the men in the line, and turning, I saw that the last man of us was on his hands and knees in the sand, with his head lowered. I ran to him. Sticking from the side of his back was a great goose-shaft, the feather and some three inches of the wood showing; and when I raised him till he came to his knees, I saw the point coming out at his armpit, for he wore no back-plate. We laid him on his side under the rocks and waited till he died. It was not long; he rolled himself as I have seen an acrobat do, talking hastily of small affairs of our old hall. So we left him on the sand and tramped on under the rocks. We turned a point where the beach ran out a little and the great waves reared themselves like angry clouds, on end, and then another man fell with a sharp sound as of the bird who pecks on the side of trees. It was a cross-bow bolt that had hit him in the side of the head. Even as we were turning from him the man next to me gave a sharp cry and put his hand on my shoulder, and pointing upwards to the heights above, spoke in a trembling voice, "They have found us." He had a long arrow shot through his right forearm just above the wrist, where there was a space between his leather glove and the sleeve of his chain-shirt. Then we went on, with him cursing and groaning and he pulled off his glove and emptied the blood on the sand, and it dripped from his fingers as he plodded along leaning on my shoulder. Then another man fell, this time quite dead, shot between back and breastplate, for he had no chain-shirt. Then the four of us, one behind the other hurried cursing along the narrow beach, catching occasional glimpses as we glanced upward, of brown and grey figures running, against the torn clouds of the moving sky. Soon another man fell, shot through the leg and not able to walk. There was no carrying him, and we could not leave him there, for there is torture for the sacking of churches and burning of towns and the razing of homesteads; so we told him this; and he asked us to lift him and bring him and put him in the edge of the sea where the white foam would break over him; and we did so and drew back and stood in silence. In a moment he turned to us, and with a word—"Farewell"!—he drew his dagger, and as the green of the surf curved over him I saw it go under his shoulder that he had bared, and when the green of the wave had changed to the retreating, and whispering spume again, there was only something dark in the wash of the water. Then we three others left that place and staggered on over the sucking sands. There was a headland before us, from which great fragments of rock had fallen and blocked the beach, and we could hear the sea dashing and roaring and moaning among the hollows, and see the great waves strike and leap up and scatter in sunlit spray. When we saw this bar across our path our hopes sank low, and we hurried that we might die like men or perchance get over it, and ever as we followed the curve of the beach the sputter of cross-bow bolts came from the sand behind us, and twice long arrows whizzed from my breastplate and glittered into the sea. At last we came to the rocks. I went first, climbing, my sword in my hand as a staff. We fell over the great blocks of dripping black, and we slimed our hands and armour on the seaweed that lifted with every wave; our clothes were heavy with water, and the wounded man who leant on my shoulder groaned as I hoisted him up and down. At last we gained the top of the largest rock, the outermost black fragment on which the great waves rent themselves. I knew we must not linger, and sliding down the side with my other companion, I turned for the wounded man, but he sat upon the rock his face drawn all sideways with pain, for he had raised his helmet for breath, and there was a crossbow bolt sticking firmly out from one of his eyes. One glance was all; then the world was a green fairyland with rushing music and the noise of mighty crowds; then a soft rolling as in tons of fleece, and then the air again, and sunlight.

The rock was bare. We staggered up, and crawling over stones like children before they have learned to walk, came at last to the sands again, the seaweed hanging from our shoulders and a weight as of leaden anchors driving us down.

We pressed the water from our eyes and turned and looked at each other, and then turned to the beach again; and gave a great shout, for our ship lay high on the sand, and we could see the heads of our men over the bulwark already watching us; then an arm waved, and down the gale came a fine sound of welcome in our own language. Heavy as we were we could not run, but we stumbled forward as an old horse to stable, and after we had crossed the beach, without a sound my companion fell against me, and when I held him from me and held him up, and saw the goose-shaft through his neck, I dropped him on the sands, and, cursing as I hobbled, broke into a shambling trot, using my sword as I ran. The arrows struck against my backplate as I bent over, but I had no time to look above, and the cross-bow bolts whizzed and volleyed past my ears, and sang, but I came to the ship at last and was lifted in, for I could not climb myself, and there I fell down between two of the rowers' benches and hid my face in my hands, while the arrows sang over us from the cliffs and the men looked up wondering as they crouched inside the bulwarks.

The Last Voyage

But soon they came and whispered to me for news of the expedition, and when I told them that of our lord and his forty men I only would stand before them, they groaned as men who have no to-morrow and who know not what to do. This could not go on. The bow of the ship was feathered with arrows and they began to strike into the benches and the after-deck.

"Can we not shove off?" I asked.

"Look at the sea," answered the oar-captain pointing; and as he pointed, his hand was broken by a cross-bow bolt. "I shall never hold oar again," he said. No more.

While they were binding his hand, I crept to the bulwark, and raising a shield between my head and the cliffs, looked past the stern of the ship at the white waters that reached for us, and the brown arms that opened to us, and I thought of the suffocation of the sea and of its indifference in its anger, and of its beautiful white carelessness, as I went down—down—down—to the bottom-most seaweeds, where the eyeless cold things crawl.

I was very weak; now they brought me meat and strong, flame-coloured water to drink; and the meat did me much good, but the flame-coloured water sent me to sleep under one of the forward benches, out of the arrows' flight. And when I waked a new dawn was breaking, and I heard the shouting of men outside the ship, the shouting of men in the language of those countries; and I lifted my sick head and gazed at them, but they curved and numbered and unnumbered themselves, till at last I heard in my brain a twanging of bows, and looking upward to the fore-deck, I saw our few men gathered there, crouching, and sending their arrows fast. The sea had not gone down, but the wind did not whistle, and in the west the clouds looked like heavy rain and thunder. As the mist that is over the sea-beach in those countries in the morning cleared off, I looked again, and I found that the men who disputed with us from the beach were few, they being but six knights in half-armour. Now, lying and watching, for I felt that I could do nothing till the world was level again, I saw the fifteen of our men jump from the fore-deck at a word from the oar-captain, and thrusting the long oars over the sides, strain on them in the sand as each wave came in, and as they strained upon them the ship would lift and glide out more, and faster; till at last we were quite afloat and the great waves took us, and turned us about, like a piece of bark. Then the men fell into their places and we headed the white seas, the half-armed men on the beach riding knee-high on their horses into the foam, and calling curses at us. So, after weary rowing, and every man of us wet as the sea, we came out of that bay and rode the great smooth waves that had been white the day before.

Well, we kept far from the land, only seeing, one dusk, a white cliff on our right from a distance; then the gale took us again and drove us westward and then northward, till the men would throw down their oars and cry out to the gods of the sea, to say which one of them should be sacrificed to their hate.

We were half mad with the drink we had in the ship—for we had no beer—and as we lurched and swayed in the depth beween two seas, or as we climbed up sideways and balanced for a moment while the foam flew and then surged down with sick motion, the men would trail their oars on the water and sink their heads on the handles. So, for many days we were driven as the wizards drive the storm-ships across the face of the icy moon, as the waves kiss her wet sides and the clouds break over her. So northward we went, till the cold struck into our bones and we ate fried fat like the savages of Finland; and we passed great ice-fields sometimes, at night, when the moon shone on them for miles and gave them smoothness which the sun took all away again, and made them grey and rugged and small.

Still we went north; our water was almost gone and we had only the devil's drinks, and the wet bread and fish. Now, when we passed the ice-fields the oar-captain would order us to fasten to them, and we would bring into the ship great chunks of ice and melt them in the cauldron by the mast-foot. But there came a time when for three days we saw no ice and the men's tongues were stiff for thirst. Their eyes looked cruel and sad. Thus, one night, as I lay at my place under the forward seat, wrapped in a bear-skin, I saw the black figure of a man on the rail at the other side of the ship. He crept to where the rail ends in the lift of the fore-deck. Then, dropping to the bench under which I lay, he crawled to the cauldron where a little water was left, and putting in his hand he broke off, little by little, pieces, until I could see by the long time that his hand rested in the cauldron that there was no more there. Then I reached out and grasped him by the leg and pulling him off the bench I rolled myself about him and called out for the oar-captain. The oar-captain came and all the men came after and they lit a light, and I lay off him, and we saw his face; and the oar-captain said—and to every man it seemed just—

"You have stolen the last of our

water, more than your share, therefore you shall go to join your comrades under the sea; when you are ready."

The man drew himself up and walked the length of the ship stepping from bench to bench, we all following, our feet making a clatter as we went. He came to the upper-deck and climbed up, and went to the rail and stood there and looked on the moveless sea under the moonlight.

"Are you ready?" asked the oar-captain.

"Get out your oars," answered the man.

Some half of the men went to their places and shoved the oars out.

"When I go, row!" he said, in a loud voice.

Then, climbing across the bulwark, he stood at the edge a moment his hands on his hips, then suddenly he raised his clenched fists in the air, and in perfect silence met the sea. As we rowed away, we could see his dark head in the moonlight as he swam, and until we had shifted the position of the ship many times we could not lose it, as the men rowed on, the oars creaking, and the indifferent moonlight silvering their slow dips.

. . . .

We are bound in by the ice, and the ship lies high in the bow, white, like a lord's tomb in the snow. It has been snowing all day, and the oar-captain makes us tramp one after the other round the half-buried ship till we can walk no more, when we sleep in the skins under the fore-deck till a comrade shakes us, and we groan and rouse and walk again. The dull sky has turned to the colour of ashes. Sometimes the air lifts for a moment into a slight wind that sends the frost-lace scurrying over the ice-blocks, and then falls still again. Our feet leave great tracks; we can hardly see through the white drift, we are silent in the wonderful white feathers ... and the silence!

Lars puffs near me, swinging his arms. The Icelander is staring out into the storm, with his hands thrust into his belt. When at last we rest in our furs, we are huddled, leaning, against one another for warmth. We cannot see the sun-set; only a dying-out of the pale half-light of the snow-drift. The men grow superstitious, and begin to talk of robbing churches, and making no restitution to the widows of killed men; and they mutter about old days—talking crossly of things we have long forgotten.

On the third night, Kai, a good man, died; on the fourth night three other men, on the fifth night, none; on the sixth day we had eaten the last of our fish, and Rudolf of Schleswig went out into the mist with his cross-bow to see if he could find anything. So, we lost him, for though he was a very strong man he never came back. It was on this same day that one of the men, Hans, a man from the south countries, little liked, went mad, and became a child again, till he wandered off and I think killed himself by a fall from a great ice-block, for we saw his black figure there, and then we heard a sound as of something striking on the ice; then more men died, I do not know, until old Olē, the oar-captain, and I only were left strong. The rest ate snow and wandered off cursing the sacking of churches or prattling nonsense of house affairs; sometimes they would come back, but I do not know if I spoke to them, for they were very dim.

It was some time in the light, when, after sitting against the side of the ship for a few moments I got up to walk again, that I saw come hopping toward me over the snow a white rabbit with white eyes.

He hops almost to my feet and then jumps into the ship; then comes a snowball rolling itself, of the height of a small man, and when it comes just before me it breaks into smoke and I cannot see through the smoke for a moment.

Music—light music, daintily, faintly playing. . . . It comes from far away . . . it is just over my head . . . then it tinkles, trills, breaks, and jingles, and falls down into the inside of my head making darkness. Now comes a long waste of clouds over the snow-fields, and the ship seems to rise to them as they billow under her bows.

They come, innumerable long fat white clouds; clouds of no shape; clouds that I hate.

I awake; I am leaning against the side of the ship; I stagger; we are tramping on the old path. A fine snow sifts down into my neck; my skin is so hot and my bones are so cold. There is no sky, only something that moves above there. Then, as I turn to the stern of the ship, I seem to hear in the distance the sound of great drinking, and the echoing of the warm beer-tankards as they strike in the air, and there comes a small and weak voice beyond me neither above nor below:

"I am Odin, the thunder-holder, and I speak to you greeting, thus, passing on."

And again the voice comes as I lean against the ship with my arms outspread.

"I am Thor, of the hammer; hail to you, man, passing on."

The sounds of the mirth of the gods die down. Then a voice speaks deeply, with no ringing in it as was in the voice of Thor, and I do not understand. The snow comes driving into my eyes, and the ship seems to lean toward me, and then away again, then all is still.

The snow comes into my eyes again, and I hear faint music as of churches and sweet voices singing, and it seems to me when I can see again that there are dim ships before me; ships whose names only I have learnt from scanty books no more; and all those gods come dancing toward me; then the music breaks, and there is great cracking of the ice, and I fall down. There is no voice of Christian God, for I have sacked his churches. The snow is in my eyes, and I am mad. I lean my head against the ship. There is no warmth, and I am afraid, alone.

THE END.

www.ingramcontent.com/pod-product-compliance
Lightning Source LLC
Chambersburg PA
CBHW020302170426
43202CB00008B/470